CompTIA CySA+

EXAM CODE CS0-001

250+ Practice Questions

www.ipspecialist.net

Document Control

Proposal Name	:	CompTIA CySA+ (CSO-001)
Document Version	:	1.0
Document Release Date	:	28-Oct-19
Reference	:	

Feedback:
If you have any comments regarding the quality of this book, or otherwise alter it to better suit your needs, you can contact us through email at info@ipspecialist.net
Please make sure to include the book title and ISBN in your message.

About IPSpecialist

IPSPECIALIST LTD. IS COMMITTED TO EXCELLENCE AND DEDICATED TO YOUR SUCCESS.

Our philosophy is to treat our customers like family. We want you to succeed, and we are willing to do everything possible to help you make it happen. We have the proof to back up our claims. We strive to accelerate billions of careers with great courses, accessibility, and affordability. We believe that continuous learning and knowledge evolution are the most important things to keep re-skilling and up-skilling the world.
Planning and creating a specific goal is where IPSpecialist helps. We can create a career track that suits your visions as well as develop the competencies you need to become a professional Network Engineer. We can also assist you with the execution and evaluation of your proficiency level, based on the career track you choose, as they are customized to fit your specific goals.
We help you STAND OUT from the crowd through our detailed IP training content packages.

Course Features:

- Self-Paced Learning
  - Learn at your own pace and in your own time
- Covers Complete Exam Blueprint
  - Prep-up for the exam with confidence
- Case Study Based Learning
  - Relate the content with real life scenarios
- Subscriptions that Suits You
  - Get more and pay less with IPS subscriptions
- Career Advisory Services
  - Let the industry experts plan your career journey
- Virtual Labs to test your skills
  - With IPS vRacks, you can evaluate your exam preparations
- Practice Questions
  - Practice questions to measure your preparation standards
- On Request Digital Certification
  - On request digital certification from IPSpecialist LTD.

About the Authors:

This book has been compiled with the help of multiple professional engineers. These engineers specialize in different fields e.g. Networking, Security, Cloud, Big Data, IoT etc. Each engineer develops content in his/her own specialized field that is compiled to form a comprehensive certification guide.

About the Technical Reviewers:

Nouman Ahmed Khan

AWS-Architect, CCDE, CCIEX5 (R&S, SP, Security, DC, Wireless), CISSP, CISA, CISM, Nouman Ahmed Khan is a Solution Architect working with a major telecommunication provider in Qatar. He works with enterprises, mega-projects, and service providers to help them select the best-fit technology solutions. He also works as a consultant to understand customer business processes and helps select an appropriate technology strategy to support business goals. He has more than fourteen years of experience working in Pakistan/Middle-East & UK. He holds a Bachelor of Engineering Degree from NED University, Pakistan, and M.Sc. in Computer Networks from the UK.

Abubakar Saeed

Abubakar Saeed has more than twenty-five years of experience, managing, consulting, designing, and implementing large-scale technology projects, extensive experience heading ISP operations, solutions integration, heading Product Development, Pre-sales, and Solution Design. Emphasizing on adhering to Project timelines and delivering as per customer expectations, he always leads the project in the right direction with his innovative ideas and excellent management skills.

Muhammad Yousuf

Muhammad Yousuf is a professional technical content writer. He is a Certified Ethical Hacker (v10) and Cisco Certified Network Associate in Routing and Switching, holding a Bachelor's Degree in Telecommunication Engineering from Sir Syed University of Engineering and Technology. He has both technical knowledge and industry sounding information, which he uses perfectly in his career.

Ayesha Sheikh

Ayesha Sheikh is a professional technical content writer. She is bronze medallist holding a Bachelor's Degree in Computer Engineering from Sir Syed University of Engineering & Technology. She has hands on experience on SDN (Software Defined Network), Java, .NET development, machine learning, PHP, Artificial Intelligence, Python and other programming and development platforms. She is an excellent research analyst and is capable of performing all her tasks in a fast and efficient way.

Shaheena Sehar

Shaheena Sehar Rafiuddin is a Technical content writer possessing a Bachelor's Degree in Telecommunication Engineering from Sir Syed University of Engineering & Technology with strong educational background. She also possesses a Master's Degree in Telecommunication Engineering from NED University of Engineering & Technology that adds more to her writing and researching capabilities.

Farah Qadir

Farah Qadir is a professional technical content writer, holding a Bachelor's Degree in Telecommunication Engineering from Sir Syed University of Engineering and Technology. With strong educational background, she possesses exceptional researching and writing skills that has led her to impart knowledge through her professional career.

Free Resources:

With each workbook bought from Amazon, IPSpecialist offers free resources to our valuable customers.

Once you buy this book, you will have to contact us at support@ipspecialist.net or tweet @ipspecialistoff to get this limited time offer without any extra charges.

Free Resources Include:

Exam Practice Questions in Quiz Simulation: With more than 250+ Q/A, IPSpecialist's Practice Questions is a concise collection of important topics to keep in mind. The questions are especially prepared following the exam blueprint to give you a clear understanding of what to expect from the certification exam. It goes further on to give answers with thorough explanations. In short, it is a perfect resource that helps you evaluate your preparation for the exam.

Career Report: This report is a step by step guide for a novice who wants to develop his/her career in the field of computer networks. It answers the following queries:

- What are the current scenarios and future prospects?
- Is this industry moving towards saturation or are new opportunities knocking at the door?
- What will the monetary benefits be?
- Why get certified?
- How to plan and when will I complete the certifications if I start today?
- Is there any career track that I can follow to accomplish specialization level?

Furthermore, this guide provides a comprehensive career path towards being a specialist in the field of networking and also highlights the tracks needed to obtain certification.

IPS Personalized Technical Support for Customers: Good customer service means helping customers efficiently, in a friendly manner. It is essential to be able to handle issues for customers and do your best to ensure they are satisfied. Providing good service is one of the most important things that can set our business apart from the others of its kind.

Great customer service will result in attracting more customers and attain maximum customer retention.

IPS is offering personalized TECH support to customers in order to provide better value for money. If you have any queries related to technology and labs you can simply ask our technical team for assistance via Live Chat or Email.

Our Products

Technology Workbooks

IPSpecialist Technology workbooks are the ideal guides to developing the hands-on skills necessary to pass the exam. Our workbook covers official exam blueprint and explains the technology with real life case study based labs. The content covered in each workbook consists of individually focused technology topics presented in an easy-to-follow, goal-oriented, step-by-step approach. Every scenario features detailed breakdowns and thorough verifications to help you completely understand the task and associated technology.

We extensively used mind maps in our workbooks to visually explain the technology. Our workbooks have become a widely used tool to learn and remember the information effectively.

vRacks

Our highly scalable and innovative virtualized lab platforms let you practice the IP Specialist Technology Workbook at your own time and your own place as per your convenience.

Quick Reference Sheets

Our quick reference sheets are a concise bundling of condensed notes of the complete exam blueprint. It is an ideal and handy document to help you remember the most important technology concepts related to the certification exam.

Practice Questions

IPSpecialists' Practice Questions are dedicatedly designed from a certification exam perspective. The collection of these questions from our technology workbooks are prepared keeping the exam blueprint in mind covering not only important but necessary topics as well. It is an ideal document to practice and revise for your certification.

CompTIA Certifications

CompTIA certification program is a vendor-neutral certification program that recognizes the best certifications in IT world. From the beginning till now CompTIA launched more than two million certifications. These certifications help you to develop a career in IT fundament by approving the hands-on skills required to troubleshoot, configure, and manage both wired and wireless networks.

CompTIA Cybersecurity Analyst (CySA+) provides accessible explanations and real-world knowledge about the exam objectives that make up the Cybersecurity Analyst+ certification. This book will help you to assess your knowledge before taking the exam, as well as provide a stepping-stone to further learning in areas where you may want to expand your skillset or expertise.

CompTIA certifications are grouped by skill set. Currently, CompTIA certifications fall into four areas: Core, Infrastructure, Cybersecurity and Additional Professional. The certification of CompTIA Cybersecurity Analyst (CySA+) lies in the Cyber Security Level area.

How does CompTIA certifications help?

These certifications are a de facto standard in networking industry, which helps you boost your career in the following ways:

1. Gets your foot in the door by launching your IT career
2. Boosts your confidence level

Proves knowledge which helps improve employment opportunities

1. Gets your foot in the door
2. Screen job applicants
3. Validate the technical skills of the candidate
4. Ensure quality, competency, and relevancy
5. Improves organization credibility and customer's loyalty
6. Helps in Job retention and promotion

About CompTIA CySA+ Exam

The CompTIA Cybersecurity Analyst (CySA+) composite exam (cso-001) is a 165-minute, Maximum of 85 question assessment that is associated with the Cybersecurity Analyst (CySA+) certification. This exam tests verifies that successful candidates have the knowledge and skills required to configure and use threat detection tools, perform data analysis and interpret the results to identify vulnerabilities, threats and risks to an organization, with the end goal of securing and protecting applications and systems within an organization.

Exam Number:	CSo-001
Associated Certifications:	Cybersecurity Analyst (CySA+)
Duration:	165 minutes (85 questions)
Available Languages:	English
Registration:	Pearson VUE

Practice Questions

1. During the reconnaissance phase, Elizabeth needs to gather information about the target organization's network infrastructure without causing an IPS to alert the target of her activities. Select a suitable procedure that Elizabeth should follow.
    A. Use a Nmap ping sweep
    B. Perform a DNS brute-force attack
    C. Use a Nmap stealth scan
    D. Perform a DNS zone transfer

Answer: **B**

Explanation: While it may seem strange, a DNS brute-force attack that queries a list of IPs, common subdomains, or other lists of targets will often bypass intrusion detection and prevention systems that do not pay particular attention to DNS queries. Elizabeth may even be able to find a DNS server that is not protected by the organization's IPS. Nmap scans are commonly used during reconnaissance, and Elizabeth can expect them to be detected since they are harder to conceal. Elizabeth should not expect to perform a zone transfer, and if she can, a well-configured IPS should immediately flag the event.

2. Emily wants to deploy an anti-malware tool to detect zero-day malware. Which of the following type of detection method should she look for in her selected tool?
    A. Availability-based
    B. Trend-based
    C. Heuristic-based
    D. Signature-based

Answer: **C**

Explanation: Heuristic detection methods run the potential malware application and track what occurs. This can allow the anti-malware tool to determine whether the behaviors and actions of the program match those common to malware, even if the file does not match the fingerprint of known malware packages.

3. John discovers a workstation during a port scan of his network that shows the following ports open. What should his next action be?

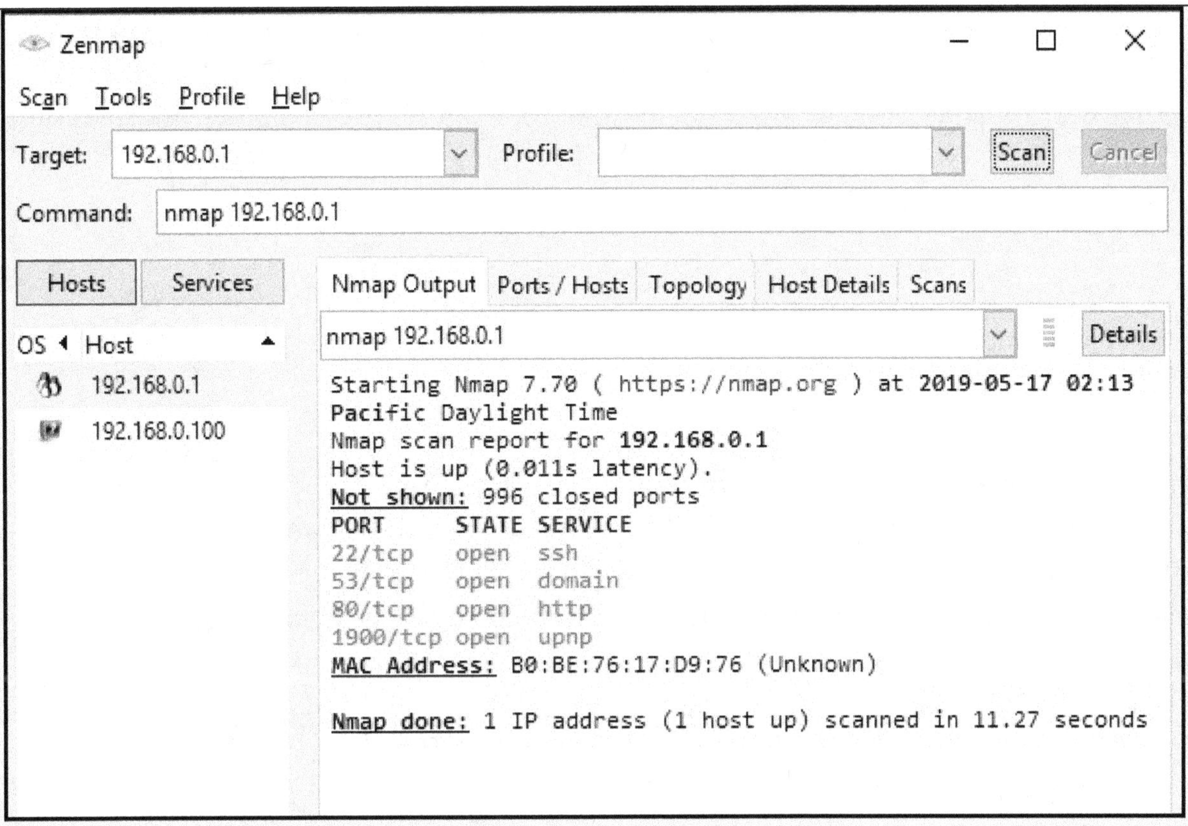

A. Re-enable the workstation's local host firewall
B. Run a vulnerability scan to identify vulnerable services
C. Investigate the potentially compromised workstation
D. Determine the reason for the ports being open

Answer: **D**

Explanation: John's first action should be to determine whether there is a legitimate reason for the workstation to have the listed ports open.

4. Which of the following term is often used for attackers?
   A. Black Team
   B. Red Team
   C. Blue Team
   D. Green Team

Answer: **B**

Explanation: Red teams are attackers, blue teams are defenders, and the white teams establish the rules of engagement and performance metrics for the test.

5. During a network reconnaissance exercise, William gains access to a computer located in a secure network. If William wants to locate database and web servers that the company uses, what command-line tool can he use to gather information about other systems on the local network without installing additional tools or sending additional traffic?
   A. Netstat
   B. Nmap
   C. Traceroute
   D. Ping

Answer: **A**

Explanation: Netstat is found on Windows, Linux, and macOS systems. It can provide information about other systems on the network and information about open ports and systems that the host has connected to. William can search for common web and database server service ports to help identify the local targets he is looking for.

6. John wants to grab the banner from a remote web server by usually using available tools. Which of the following tools cannot be used to grab the banner from the remote host?
   A. wget
   B. ftp
   C. netcat
   D. telnet

Answer: **B**

Explanation: netcat, telnet, and wget can all be used to conduct John's banner-grabbing exercise. FTP will not connect properly to get the banner he wants to see.

7. Elizabeth needs to conduct a passive footprinting exercise against a target company. Which of the following techniques is not suitable for a passive footprinting process?
   A. BGP Looking Glass Usage
   B. Registrar Checks
   C. WHOIS Lookups
   D. Banner Grabbing

Answer: **D**

Explanation: Banner grabbing is an active process and requires a connection to a remote host to grab the banner.

8. Emily has been asked to assess the likelihood of reconnaissance activities against her organization (a small, regional business). Her first assignment is to determine the likelihood of port scans against systems in her organization's DMZ. How should she rate the likelihood of this occurring?
   A. High
   B. Low
   C. Medium
   D. None of the above

Answer: **A**

Explanation: Emily knows that systems that are exposed to the internet like DMZ systems are constantly being scanned. She should rate the likelihood of the scan occurring as high. In fact, there is a good chance that a scan will be occurring while she is typing up her report.

9. John configures an alert that detects when users who do not typically travel log in from other countries. Which of the following type of analysis is this?
   A. Behavior
   B. Heuristic
   C. Availability
   D. Trend

Answer: **A**

Explanation: John has configured a behavior-based detection. It is likely that a reasonable percentage of the detections will be for legitimate travel for users who typically do not leave the country, but pairing this behavioral detection with other behavioral or anomaly detections can help determine whether the login is legitimate.

10. During his analysis of a malware sample, John reviews the malware files and binaries without running them. What type of analysis is this?
   A. Dynamic
   B. Static
   C. Automated
   D. Heuristic

Answer: **B**

Explanation: John is performing static analysis that analysis is performed without running code. He can use tools or manually review the code (and, in fact, is likely to do both).

11. Which of the following tools can be used to passively gather the information required to generate a network topology map?
    A. Nessus
    B. SolarWinds Network Mapper
    C. Nmap
    D. Wireshark

Answer: **D**

Explanation: Wireshark can be used to capture network traffic, allowing you to review traffic information to build a network topology based on time to live, IP addresses, and other information. Nmap and SolarWinds Network Mapper both rely on active scans to generate topologies, and Nessus does not provide a network topology generation capability.

12. Which of the following type of control review will focus on change management as a major element in its assessment scope?
    A. Technical Control Review
    B. Detective Control Review
    C. Operational Control Review
    D. Responsive Control Review

Answer: **C**

Explanation: A review of operational controls will often look at change management, separation of duties and other personnel controls, and process-based controls. Many administrative controls are part of an operational control review.

13. Select one from the following that provides a standardized way to name Nmap hardware and software that it detects.
    A. HardwareEnum
    B. CVE
    C. GearScript
    D. CPE

Answer: **D**

Explanation: Nmap's Common Platform Enumeration is a standardized way to name applications, operating systems, and hardware.

14. John wants to list all of the NetBIOS sessions open on a workstation. What command should he issue to do this?
    A. nbtstat -s
    B. nbtstat –c
    C. nbtstat -o
    D. nbtstat -r

Answer: **A**

Explanation: To show current NetBIOS sessions and their status, John can issue the nbtstat -s command. The -c flag shows the NetBIOS name cache, while the -r command displays the count of NetBIOS names resolved through a WINS server query and by broadcast. There is no -o flag.

15. William is responsible for hardening systems on his network. He discovers that a number of network appliances have exposed services including telnet, FTP, and web servers. What is the best option to secure these systems?
    A. Place a network firewall between the devices and the rest of the network
    B. Install patches for those services
    C. Turn off the services for each appliance
    D. Enable host firewalls

Answer: **A**

Explanation: William's only sure bet to prevent these services from being accessed is to put a network firewall in front of them. Many appliances enable services by default; since they are appliances, they may not have host firewalls available to be enabled. They also often do not have patches available, and many do not allow the services they provide to be disabled or modified.

16. While reviewing email logs for his domain's email server, John notices that a single remote host is sending emails to usernames that appear to be in alphabetical order:

root@kali: ~
File Edit View Search Terminal Help
[*] pistolsales@hotmail.com
[*] plombiren@hotmail.com
[*] pstout@hotmail.com
[*] remcostam@hotmail.com
[*] rozsii@hotmail.com
[*] rraymond80@hotmail.com
[*] ruth.dee@hotmail.com
[*] salon.eli@hotmail.com
[*] sanjaya3@hotmail.com
[*] satisjenie2@hotmail.com
[*] shahidhussainghauri@hotmail.com
[*] sickwited1@hotmail.com
[*] someone@hotmail.com
[*] total_bottom@hotmail.com
[*] username@hotmail.com
[*] vigor_58@hotmail.com
[*] wilfred.7@hotmail.com
[*] wxac@hotmail.com
[*] xxxxxx@hotmail.com
[*] z3ka-14@hotmail.com
[*] Writing email address list to emailharvest.txt...
[*] Auxiliary module execution completed
msf5 auxiliary(gather/search_email_collector) > use gather/search-email-collecte

This behavior continues for thousands of entries, resulting in many bounced email messages, but some make it through. What type of reconnaissance has John encountered?

A. Email Harvesting
B. Brute Force
C. Email List Builder
D. Domain Probe

Answer: **A**

Explanation: This type of probe is known as domain harvesting and it relies on message rejection error messages to help the individual running the probe to determine which email accounts actually exist. John may want to disable delivery receipts, disable non-deliverable responses, or investigate more advanced techniques like false non-deliverable responses or recipient filtering and tar pitting.

17. Which of the following capabilities is not a typical part of a SIEM system?
    A. Alerting
    B. Log Retention
    C. Data Aggregation

D. Performance Management

Answer: **D**

Explanation: SIEM systems typically provide alerting, event and log correlation, compliance data gathering and reporting, data and log aggregation, and data retention capabilities. This also means that they can be used for forensic analysis as they should be designed to provide a secure copy of data.

18. Which of the three key objectives of cybersecurity is often ensured by using techniques like hashing and the use of tools like Tripwire?
    A. Integrity
    B. Confidentiality
    C. Identification
    D. Availability

Answer: **A**

Explanation: The three objectives of cybersecurity are confidentiality, integrity, and availability. Hashing and the use of integrity monitoring tools like Tripwire are both techniques used to preserve integrity; in fact, file integrity monitoring tools typically use hashing to verify that files remain intact and unchanged.

19. An access control system that relies on the operating system to constrain the ability of a subject to execute operations is an example of which type of access control system?
    A. A role-based access control system
    B. A discretionary access control system
    C. A level-based access control system
    D. A mandatory access control system

Answer: **D**

Explanation: A mandatory access control system relies on the operating system to constrain what actions or access a subject that can perform on an object. Role-based access control uses roles to determine access to resources, and discretionary access control allows subjects to control access to objects that they own or are responsible for. Level-based access control is a type of role-based access control.

20. John received a pcap file from a system administrator at a remote site who was concerned about the traffic it showed. Which of the following type of behavior

should John report after his analysis of the file?

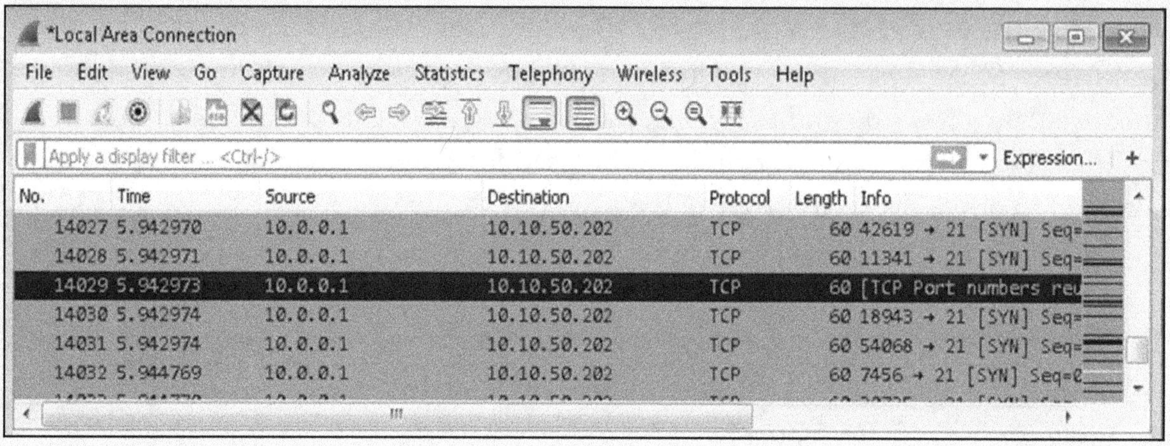

A. DOS Attack
B. DDoS Attack
C. Port Scanning
D. Service Access Issues

Answer: **C**

Explanation: John may immediately notice that all traffic comes from one host (10.100.25.14) and is sent to the same host (10.100.18.12). All the traffic shown is TCP SYNs to well-known ports. Charles should quickly identify this as a SYN-based port scan.

21. What U.S. government program seeks to provide trusted sources that meet the following requirements?
    A. Provide a chain of custody for classified and unclassified integrated circuits
    B. Ensure that there will not be any reasonable threats related to supply disruption
    C. Prevent intentional or unintentional modification or tampering of integrated circuits
    D. Protect integrated circuits from reverse engineering and vulnerability testing
    E. Trusted Access Program
    F. Chain of Custody
    G. Trusted Suppliers
    H. Trusted Foundry

Answer: **D**

Explanation: The U.S. Department of Defense's Trusted Foundry program is intended to ensure the integrity and confidentiality of integrated circuits throughout the design and manufacturing life cycle while retaining access to leading-edge technology for trusted and untrusted uses.

22. John wants to gather as much information as he can about an organization using DNS harvesting methods. Which of the following methods will easily provide the most useful information if they are all possible to conduct on the network he is targeting?
    A. Domain Brute Forcing
    B. Reverse Lookup
    C. Zone Transfer
    D. DNS Record Enumeration

Answer: **C**

Explanation: If John can perform a zone transfer, he can gather all of the organization's DNS information, including domain servers, host names, MX and CNAME records, time to live records, zone serial number data, and other information. This is the easiest way to gather the most information about an organization via DNS if it is possible. Unfortunately, for penetration testers (and attackers), few organizations allow untrusted systems to perform zone transfers.

23. William's penetration test requires him to use passive mapping methods to discover network topology. Which of the following tools is best suited to that task?
    A. Netcat
    B. Angry IP Scanner
    C. Wireshark
    D. Nmap

Answer: **C**

Explanation: Passive network mapping can be done by capturing network traffic using a sniffing tool like Wireshark. Active scanners including nmap, the Angry IP Scanner, and netcat (with the -z flag for port scanning) could all set off alarms as they scan systems on the network.

24. Which of the following items is not one of the three important rules that should be established before a penetration test?
    A. Reporting
    B. Timing
    C. Scope
    D. Authorization

Answer: **A**

Explanation: It is critical to determine when a penetration test will occur, what systems, networks, personnel, and other targets are part of the test and which are not. In addition, testers must have the proper permission to perform the test. The content and format of the summary are important but not critical to have in place before the penetration test occurs.

25. Every year, Emily downloads and reads a security industry published a list of all the types of attacks, compromises, and malware events that have occurred, which are becoming more prevalent, and is decreasing in occurrence. Which of the following type of analysis can she perform using this information?
    A. Availability
    B. Heuristic
    C. Trend
    D. Anomaly

Answer: **C**

Explanation: Emily can use trend analysis to help her determine what attacks are most likely to target her organization and then take action based on the trends that are identified.

26. Part of Emily's penetration testing assignment is to evaluate the WPA2 Enterprise protected wireless networks of her target organization. What are the major differences existing between reconnaissance of a wired network versus a wireless network?
    A. Network Access Control and Encryption
    B. Encryption and Physical Accessibility
    C. Authentication and Encryption
    D. Port Security and Physical Accessibility

Answer: **B**

Explanation: Emily knows that most wired networks do not use end-to-end encryption by default and that wireless networks are more easily accessible than a wired network that requires physical access to a network jack or a VPN connection from an authorized account.

27. John is reviewing his team's work as part of a reconnaissance effort and is checking

Wireshark packet captures. His team reported no open ports on 10.10.50.202. What issue should he identify with their scan based on the capture shown here?

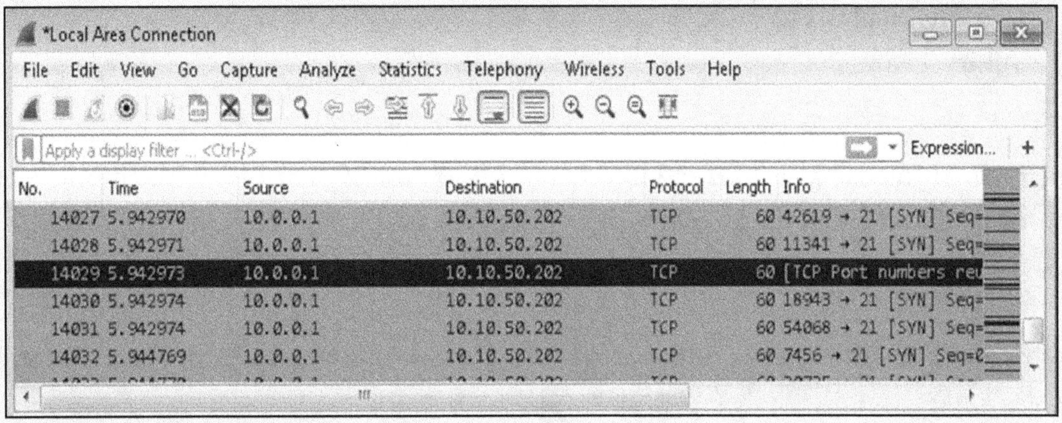

A. The host was not up
B. The scan scanned only TCP ports
C. Not all ports were scanned
D. The scan was not run as root

Answer: **B**

Explanation: This scan shows only TCP ports. Since most services run as UDP services, this scan would not have identified most common servers. John should review the commands that his team issued as part of their exercise.

28. William needs to protect his organization's authentication system against brute-force attacks. Which of the following control pairs are suitable for preventing a brute-force attack from succeeding if ease of use and maintenance is also essentials?
    A. Passwords and token-based authentication
    B. Token-based authentication and biometrics
    C. Passwords and PINs
    D. Passwords and biometrics

Answer: **A**

Explanation: A password combined with token-based authentication can prevent brute-force attacks that might succeed against a password or a password and PIN combination.

29. John has been asked to monitor and manage the environment in which a cybersecurity exercise is conducted. Which of the following team is he on?

A. Blue Team
B. Black Team
C. Red Team
D. White Team

Answer: **D**

Explanation: John is part of the white team, which manages the environment. The red team attacks, and the blue team defends. The black team is not a term that is commonly used in this context.

30. Which of the following is not included in the rules of engagement for a penetration test?
    A. Authorized Tools
    B. Scope
    C. Authorization
    D. Timing

Answer: **A**

Explanation: Authorized tools are not included in the rules of engagement. The rules of engagement for a penetration test typically describe the scope, timing, authorization, and techniques that will be used (or that are prohibited).

31. Which of the following tools is not associated with the reconnaissance stage of a penetration test?
    A. Nessus
    B. Maltego
    C. Metasploit
    D. Nmap

Answer: **C**

Explanation: Nmap, Nessus, and Maltego are all commonly used to discover information about an organization or individuals. Metasploit is primarily an exploitation tool. While it has modules that can be used for reconnaissance, it is primarily used to target discovered vulnerabilities.

32. What will occur when John uses the following command to perform a nmap scan of a network?

    nmap -sn 192.168.0.1/24

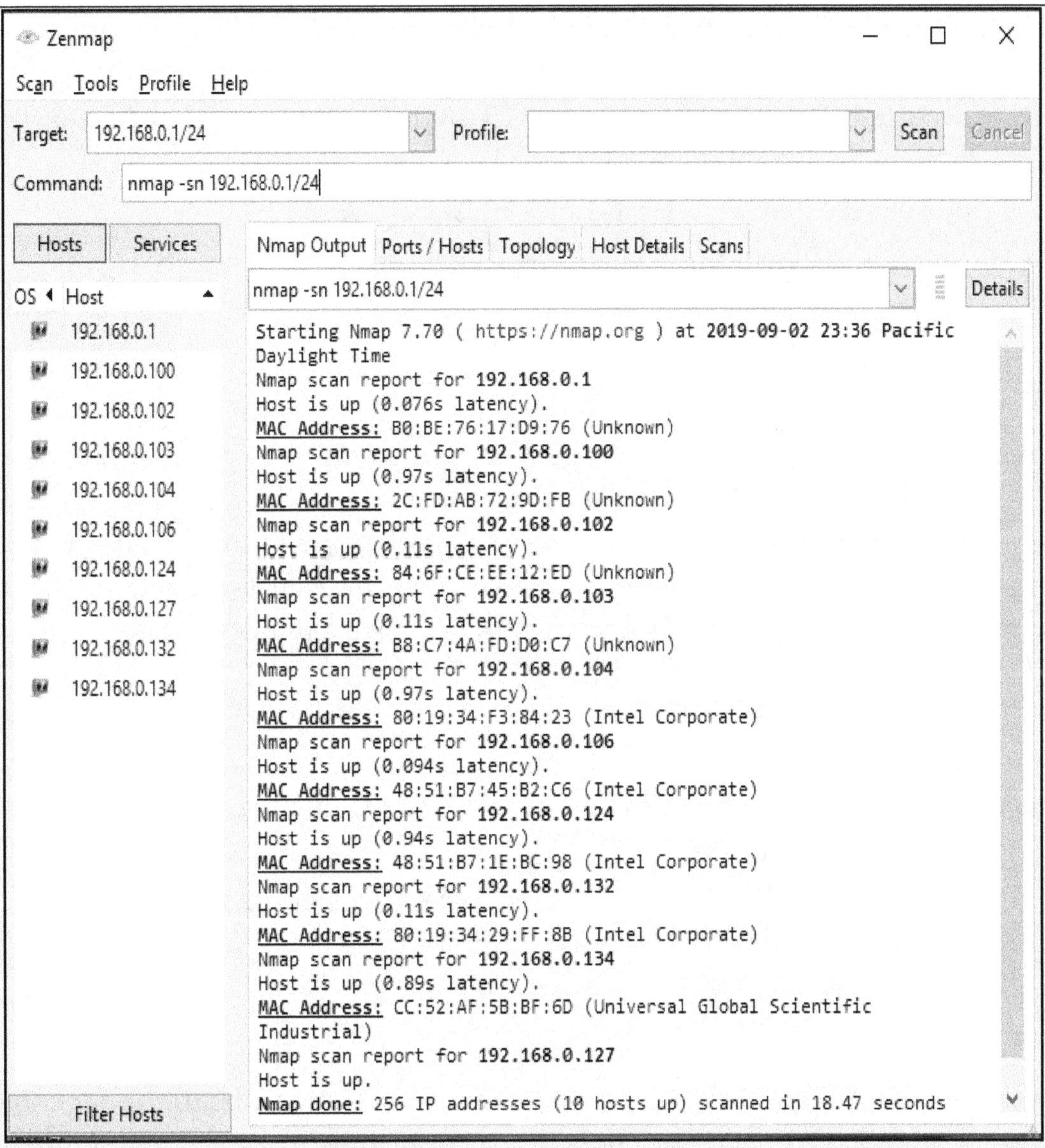

A. A SYN-based port scan of all hosts in the 192.168.2.0 to 192.168.2.255 network range
B. A scan of all hosts that respond to ping in the 192.168.0.0 to 192.168.255.255 network range
C. A scan of all hosts that respond to ping in the 192.168.0.0 to 192.168.0.255 network range
D. A secure port scan of all hosts in the 192.168.0.0 to 192.168.2.255 network range

Answer: **C**

Explanation: The -sn flag for nmap indicates a ping scan, and /24 indicates a range of 255 addresses. In this case, that means the nmap will scan for hosts that respond to ping in the 192.168.0.0 to 192.168.0.255 IP address range.

33. Why does the U.S. government require Trusted Foundry and related requirements for technology?
    A. To prevent the hardware-level compromise of devices
    B. To ensure U.S.-based supplier viability for strategic components
    C. To control prices
    D. To ensure standards compatibility

Answer: **A**

Explanation: According to the Defense Microelectronics Activity (DMEA) website: "DMEA accredits suppliers in the areas of integrated circuit design, aggregation, broker, mask manufacturing, foundry, post-processing, packaging/assembly and test services. These services cover a broad range of technologies and are intended to support both new and legacy applications, both classified and unclassified."

34. Which of the following sources are most commonly used to gather information about technologies to target organization uses during intelligence gathering?
    A. Port scanning and social engineering
    B. OSINT searches of support forums and social engineering
    C. Social engineering and document metadata
    D. Social media review and document metadata

Answer: **B**

Explanation: Since organizations often protect information about the technologies they use, searches of support forums and social engineering are often combined to gather information about the technologies they have in place.

35. You would like to determine whether any services that are available on the network devices should NOT be available. Which of the following can you use to identify this?
    A. Packet Capture
    B. Service Discovery
    C. OS Fingerprinting
    D. Topology Discovery

Answer: **B**

Explanation: Available services on a device are discovered by identifying the open ports on the device.

36. Recently, there were reports of malicious individuals attempting to take advantage of well-known vulnerabilities on certain devices. Which of the following would allow those individuals to match these well-known vulnerabilities to each device?
    A. Packet Capture
    B. Service Discovery
    C. OS Fingerprinting
    D. Topology Discovery

Answer: **C**

Explanation: By determining the operating system, the hacker may be able to take advantage of weaknesses derived from missing security patches.

37. The cyber team just received an alert from the IDS that someone is using an automated process to collect emails. Which of the following would make this possible?
    A. Service Discovery
    B. Packet Capture
    C. Harvesting Bots
    D. OS Fingerprinting

Answer: **C**

Explanation: Attackers may attempt a process called **email harvesting**, and the security analyst should attempt it as well. Typically, email harvesting bots (automated processes) are used for this.

38. The organization decided to execute its own penetration test in preparation for a test that will be performed by a compliance body. The organization needs to obtain a port scanning tool. Which of the following is one of the most popular port scanning tools used today?
    A. Nmap
    B. Nbtstat
    C. Netstat
    D. Wireshark

Answer: **A**

Explanation: After performing scans with certain flags set in the scan packets, security analysts (and hackers) can make positive assumptions based on the responses received.

39. Which of the following control types are designed to discourage an attacker?
    A. Deterrent
    B. Directive
    C. Corrective
    D. Detective

Answer: **A**

Explanation: Deterrent controls deter or discourage an attacker. Deterrent controls often generate preventive and corrective controls. Examples of deterrent controls include user identification and authentication, fences, lighting, and organizational security policies, such as a Non-Disclosure Agreement (NDA).

40. _________________ is a component to which a Group Policy can be applied.
    A. Security Groups
    B. Site
    C. Domains
    D. Organizational Units

Answer: **A**

Explanation: A security group is not a component of Active Directory. GPOs can only be applied to components of Active Directory. These include OUs, trees, and domains.

41. What is the first step in a pentest?
    A. Gather information about attack methods against the target system or device
    B. Execute attacks against the target system or device to gain user and privileged access
    C. Document the results of the penetration test
    D. Document information about the target system or device

Answer: **D**

Explanation: There are some steps in performing a penetration test, which include:

A. Document information about the target system or device.

B. Gather information about attack methods against the target system or device. This includes performing port scans.
C. Identify the known vulnerabilities of the target system or device.
D. Execute attacks against the target system or device to gain user and privileged access.
E. Document the results of the penetration test and report the findings to management, with suggestions for remedial action.

42. When performing qualitative risk evaluation, which of the following is considered in addition to the impact of the event?
A. Attack Vectors
B. Costs
C. Likelihood
D. Frequency

Answer: **C**

Explanation: An attempt must be made to establish both the likelihood of a threat's realization and the impact to the organization if it occurs.

43. If John wants to validate the application files he has downloaded from the vendor of his application, what information should he request from them?
A. The private key and cryptographic hash
B. The public key and cryptographic hash
C. File size and file creation date
D. MD5 hash

Answer: **D**

Explanation: John only needs a verifiable MD5 hash to validate the files under almost all circumstances. This will let him verify that the file he downloaded matches the hash of the file that the vendor believes they are providing.

44. The organization that William works for categorizes the security-related events using NIST's standard definitions. Which of the following classification should he use when he discovers key logging software on one of his frequent business traveler's laptop?

A. A Security Incident
B. A Policy Violation
C. An Event
D. An Adverse Event

Answer: **A**

Explanation: NIST describes events as security incidents because they are a violation or imminent threat of violation of security policies and practices.

45. Emily is designing a segmented network that places systems with different levels of security requirements into different subnets with firewalls and other network security devices between them. Which of the following phase of the incident response process is Emily in?
A. Containment, Eradication, and Recovery
B. Preparation
C. Detection and Analysis
D. Post-incident Activity

Answer: **B**

Explanation: Emily's efforts are part of the preparation phase, which involves activities intended to limit the damage an attacker could cause.

46. The company that Brian works for processes credit cards and is required to be compliant with PCI-DSS. If Brian's company experiences a breach of card data, which of the following type of disclosure, will they be required to provide?
A. Notification to federal law enforcement
B. Notification to Visa and MasterCard
C. Notification to local law enforcement
D. Notification to their acquiring bank

Answer: **D**

Explanation: Organizations that process credit cards work with acquiring banks to handle their card processing, rather than directly with the card providers. Notification to the bank is part of this type of response effort.

47. John wants to build scripts to detect malware beaconing behavior. Which of the following is not a typical means of identifying malware beaconing behavior on a

network?

A. Beacon Protocol
B. Persistence of the Beaconing
C. Removal of Known Traffic
D. Beaconing Interval

Answer: **A**

Explanation: Unless John already knows the protocol that a particular beacon uses, filtering out beacons by protocol may cause him to miss beaconing behavior. Attackers want to dodge common analytical tools and will use protocols that are less likely to attract attention.

48. Which of the following type shows the forensic investigation–related form?

A. Forensic Discovery Log
B. Policy Custody Release
C. Chain of Custody
D. Report of Examination

Answer: **C**

Explanation: This form is a sample chain of custody form. It includes information about the case, copies of drives that were created, and who was in possession of drives, devices, and copies during the investigation.

49. Emily is following the CompTIA process for validation after a compromise. Which of the following actions should be included in this phase?

A. Setting Permissions
B. Secure Disposal
C. Sanitization
D. Re-imaging

Answer: **A**

Explanation: CompTIA defines two phases: incident eradication and validation. Validation phase activities per CompTIA's split include patching, permissions, scanning, and verifying whether logging works properly.

50. John has access to a full suite of network monitoring tools and wants to use appropriate tools to monitor network bandwidth consumption. Which of the following is not a common technique of monitoring network bandwidth usage?
    A. Packet Sniffing
    B. Netflow
    C. SNMP
    D. Portmon

Answer: **D**

Explanation: SNMP, packet sniffing, and Netflow are commonly used when monitoring bandwidth consumption. Portmon is an aging Windows tool used to monitor serial ports

51. Emily is attempting to determine when a user account was created on a Windows 10 workstation. Which of the following method is her best option if she believes the account was created recently?
    A. Check the security log
    B. Query the registry for the user ID creation date
    C. Check the system log
    D. Check the user profile creation date

Answer: **A**

Explanation: If the Security log has not rotated, Emily should be able to find the account creation under event ID. The System log does not contain user creation events, and user profile information does not exist until the user's first login. The registry is also not a reliable source of account creation date information.

52. Elizabeth sees high CPU utilization in the Windows Task Manager, as shown here while reviewing a system's performance issues. If she wants to get a detailed view of the CPU usage by application, with PIDs and average CPU usage, which of the following tool can she use to gather that detail?

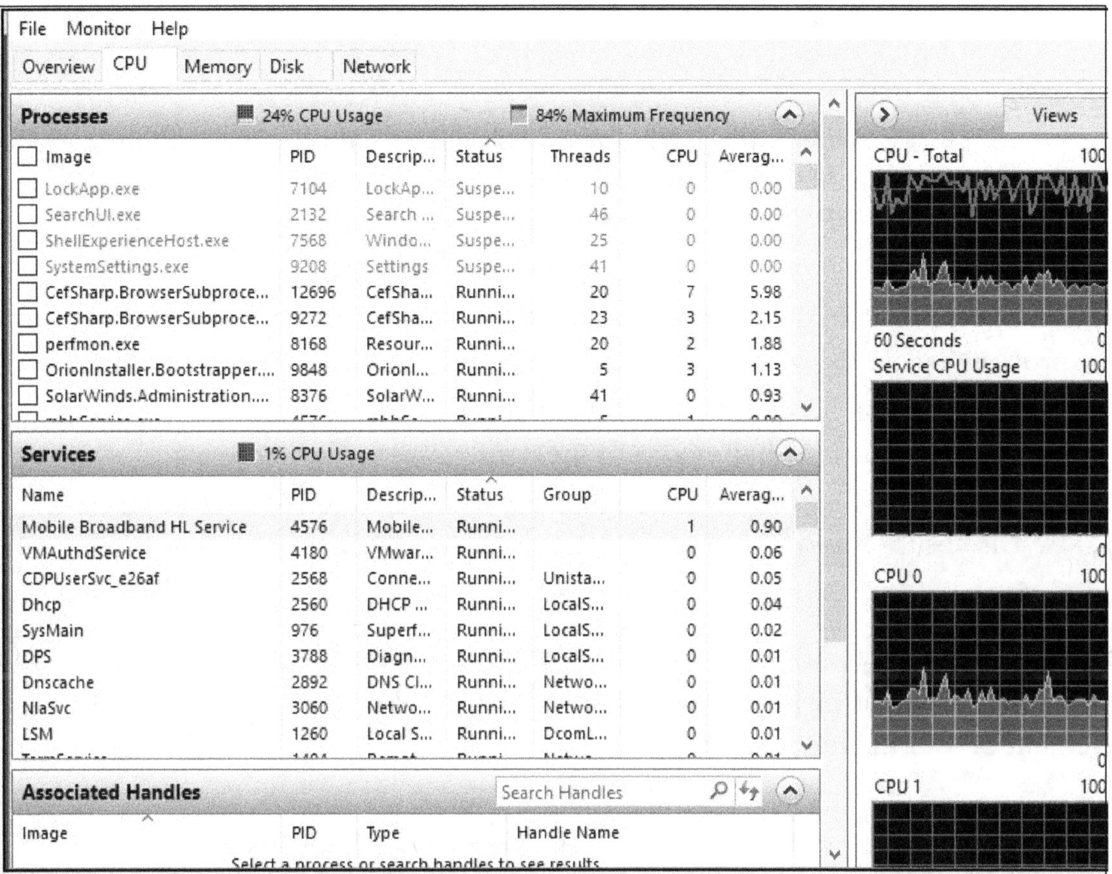

A. iperf
B. Perfmon
C. Resource Monitor
D. Task Manager

Answer: **C**

Explanation: Resource Manager provides average CPU utilization in addition to real-time CPU utilization.

53. During a forensic investigation, William records information about each drive, including where it was acquired, who made the forensic copy, the MD5 hash of the drive, and other details. Which of the following term describes the process William is using as he labels evidence with details of who acquired and validated it?
    A. Chain of Custody
    B. Incident Logging
    C. Circumstantial Evidence

D. Direct Evidence

Answer: **A**

Explanation: The chain of custody for evidence is maintained by logging and labeling evidence. This ensures that the evidence is properly controlled and accessed.

54. All the following is an important part of the incident response communication process, except for ________________________.
    A. Using a secure method of communication
    B. Preventing accidental release of incident-related information
    C. Limiting communication to trusted parties
    D. Disclosure based on public feedback

Answer: **D**

Explanation: Disclosure based on regulatory or legislative requirements is common part of an incident response process; however, public feedback is typically a guiding element of information release.

55. Amy wants to use her network security device to detect potential beaconing behavior. Which of the following options is suitable for detecting beaconing by using her network security device?
    A. Static File Analysis
    B. IP Reputation
    C. File Reputation
    D. Antivirus Definitions

Answer: **B**

Explanation: Amy's best choice would be to implement an IP reputation to monitor for connections to known bad hosts. Antivirus definitions, file reputation, and static file analysis are all useful for detecting malware.

56. During an incident response process, Elizabeth plugs a system back into the network, allowing it normal network access. Which of the following phase of the incident response process is Elizabeth performing?
    A. Detection and Analysis

B. Preparation
C. Post-incident Activity
D. Containment, Eradication, and Recovery

Answer: **D**

Explanation: Restoring a system to normal function, including removing it from isolation, is part of the containment, eradication, and recovery stage.

57. Jane's team has completed the initial phases of the incident response process and is assessing the time required to recover from the incident. Using the NIST recoverability effort categories, the team members have determined that they can predict the time to recover but will require additional resources. How should she classify this using the NIST model?
    A. Supplemented
    B. Regular
    C. Extended
    D. Not recoverable

Answer: **A**

Explanation: The NIST recoverability effort categories call a scenario in which time to recovery is predictable with an additional resources "supplemented". The key to the NIST levels is to remember that each level of additional resources required increases the severity level from regular to supplemented and then to extend.

58. John is aware that an attacker has compromised a system on his network but wants to continue to observe the attacker's efforts as the attack continues. If John wants to prevent additional impact on his network while watching what the attacker does, which of the following containment method should he use?
    A. Segmentation
    B. Detection
    C. Removal
    D. Isolation

Answer: **D**

Explanation: John can choose to isolate the compromised system, either physically or logically, leaving the attacker with access to the system while isolating it from other systems on his network. If he makes a mistake, he could leave his own systems vulnerable, but this will allow him to observe the attacker.

59. During an incident response process, Emily conducts a lessons-learned review. Which of the following phase of the incident response process is she in?
    A. Post-incident Recovery
    B. Containment, Eradication, and Recovery
    C. Detection and Analysis
    D. Preparation

Answer: **A**

Explanation: Lessons-learned reviews are conducted as part of the post-incident activity stage of incident response and they provide an opportunity for organizations to improve their incident response process.

60. During their organization's incident response preparation, John and William are identifying critical information assets that the company uses. Included in their organizational data sets is a list of customer names, addresses, phone numbers, and demographic information. How should John and William classify this information?
    A. PHI
    B. PCI-DSS
    C. PII
    D. Intellectual property

Answer: **C**

Explanation: Personally Identifiable Information (PII) includes information that can be used to identify, contact, or locate a specific individual.

61. What is the main role of management in the incident response process?
    A. Assessing the impact on stakeholders
    B. Providing authority and resources
    C. Acting as the primary interface with law enforcement
    D. Leading the CSIRT(Computer Security Incident Response Team)

Answer: **B**

Explanation: The main role of management in an incident response effort is to provide the authority and resources required to respond appropriately to the incident.

62. NIST describes four major phases in the incident response cycle. Which of the following is not one of the four?
    A. Detection and Analysis
    B. Preparation
    C. Containment, Eradication, and Recovery
    D. Notification and Communication

Answer: **D**

Explanation: Notification and communication may occur in multiple phases. NIST identifies four major phases in the incident response life cycle, including:

A. Preparation
B. Detection and Analysis
C. Containment, Eradication, and Recovery
D. Post-incident Activity

63. NIST SP 800-61 classifies six outside parties that an incident response team will usually communicate with. This includes all of the following parties except for_________.
    A. Law Enforcement Agencies
    B. Legal Counsel
    C. Customers, Constituents, and Media
    D. Internet Service Providers

Answer: **B**

Explanation: NIST classifies customers, constituents, media, other incident response teams, internet service providers, incident reporters, law enforcement agencies, and software and support vendors as outside parties that an IR (Incident Response) team will communicate with.

64. Which of the following common incident response follow-up activity includes asking questions like "What additional tools or resources are needed to detect or analyze future events?"?
    A. Lessons-learned Review

B. Preparation
C. Procedural Analysis
D. Evidence Gathering

Answer: **A**

Explanation: Questions including what tools and resources are needed to detect, analyze, or mitigate figure incidents, as well as topics such as how information sharing could be improved, what could be done better or differently, and how effective existing processes and policies are, can all be part of the lessons-learned review.

65. During an incident response process, Emily heads to a compromised system and pulls its network cable. Which of the following phase of the incident response process is Emily performing?
    A. Post-incident Activity
    B. Containment, Eradication, and Recovery
    C. Detection and Analysis
    D. Preparation

Answer: **B**

Explanation: Removing a system from the network typically occurs as part of the containment phase of an incident response process.

66. John needs to validate that the forensic image he has created is an exact duplicate of the original drive. Which of the following techniques is considered forensically sound? (You can select more than one option)
    A. Create a MD5 hash
    B. Create a SHA-1 hash
    C. Create a SHA-2 hash
    D. None of the above

Answer: **A, B, C**

Explanation: MD5, SHA-1, and SHA-2 hashes are all considered forensically sound.

67. Which of the following strategy does NIST suggest for identifying attackers during

an incident response process?

A. Identifying attackers is not an important part of the incident response process
B. Contacting upstream ISPs for assistance in tracking down the attacker
C. Contacting local law enforcement so that they can use law enforcement–specific tools
D. Using geographic IP tracking to identify the attacker's location

Answer: **A**

Explanation: NIST's Computer Security Incident Handling Guide notes that identifying an attacker can be "time-consuming and futile". In general, spending time identifying attackers is not a valuable use of incident response time for most organizations.

68. Patents, copyrights, trademarks, and trade secrets are all related to which of the following kind of data?

A. Corporate Confidential
B. Intellectual Property
C. PII
D. PHI

Answer: **B**

Explanation: Patents, copyrights, trademarks, and trade secrets are all forms of intellectual property.

69. Elizabeth wants to check on memory, CPU, disk, network, and power usage on a Mac. Which of the following GUI tools can she use to check these?

A. Resource Monitor
B. Activity Monitor
C. System Monitor
D. Sysradar

Answer: **B**

Explanation: The built-in macOS utility for measuring memory, CPU, disk, network, and power usage in Activity Monitor.

70. As an employee of the U.S. government, Emily is required to use NIST's information impact categories to classify security incidents. During a recent incident, proprietary information was changed. How should she classify this incident?
   A. As an Availability Breach
   B. As a Proprietary Breach
   C. As an Integrity Loss
   D. As a Privacy Breach

Answer: **C**

Explanation: NIST classifies changes or deletion of sensitive or proprietary information as an integrity loss.

71. During what phase of an event is the preservation of evidence typically handled?
   A. Detection and Analysis
   B. Preparation
   C. Post-incident Activity
   D. Containment, Eradication, and Recovery

Answer: **D**

Explanation: While responders are working to contain the incident, they should also reserve forensic and incident information for future analysis. Restoration of service is often prioritized over-analysis during containment activities, but taking the time to create forensic images and to preserve log and other data is important for later investigation.

72. Profiling networks and systems can help to identify unexpected activity. Which of the following type of detection can be used once a profile has been created?
   A. Anomaly Analysis
   B. Dynamic Analysis
   C. Behavioral Analysis
   D. Static Analysis

Answer: **A**

Explanation: Profiling networks and systems will provide a baseline behavior set. A

SIEM or similar system can monitor differences or anomalies that are recorded as events.

73. Emily is conducting an incident response exercise and needs to assess the economic impact to her organization of a $500,000 expense related to an information security incident. How should she categorize this?
    A. Emily cannot assess the impact with the data given
    B. Low Impact
    C. Medium Impact
    D. High Impact

Answer: **A**

Explanation: Economic impact is calculated on a relative scale, and Emily does not have all of the information she needs. A $500,000 loss may be catastrophic for a small organization and may have a far lower impact on a Fortune 500 company. Other factors like cybersecurity insurance may also limit the economic impact of a cybersecurity incident.

74. John is responding to a ransomware incident that has encrypted financial and business data throughout the organization, including current payroll and HR data. As events currently stand, payroll cannot be run for the current pay period. If John uses the NIST functional impact categories shown the below table, how should John rate this incident?

Category	Definition
None	No effect on the organization's ability to provide all services to all users
Low	Minimal effect; the organization can still provide all critical services to all users but has lost efficiency
Medium	The organization has lost the ability to provide a critical service to a subset of system users
High	The organization is no longer able to

	provide some critical services to any users

A. Extended Recovery
B. High
C. Medium
D. Critical

Answer: **B**

Explanation: In this instance current payroll and financial data are encrypted and payroll is unable to be run, this should be categorized as a high-severity incident.

75. Emily wants to create a documented chain of custody for the systems that she is being handled as part of a forensic investigation. Which of the following will provide her with evidence that systems were not tampered with while she was not working with them?
    A. Tamper-proof Seals
    B. A Chain of Custody Log
    C. System Logs
    D. None of the above

Answer: **A**

Explanation: Tamper-proof seals are used when it is necessary to prove that devices, systems, or spaces were not accessed. They often include holographic logos that help to ensure that tampering is both visible and cannot be easily hidden by replacing the sticker.

76. William's incident response team has collected log information and is working on identifying attackers using that information. Which of the following two stages of the NIST incident response process is his time working in?
    A. Detection and Analysis, and Containment, Eradication, and Recovery
    B. Containment, Eradication, and Recovery and Post-incident Activity
    C. Preparation and Containment, Eradication, and Recovery
    D. Preparation and Post-incident Activity

Answer: **A**

Explanation: Collecting and analyzing logs most often occurs in the detection phase, while connecting attacks back to attackers is typically handled in the containment, eradication, and recovery phase of the NIST incident response process.

77. All the following activities are a part of the containment and restoration process except for ______________________.
    A. Rebuilding compromised systems
    B. Limiting service disruption
    C. Identifying the attacker
    D. Minimizing loss

Answer: **C**

Explanation: Identifying the attacker is typically handled either during the identification stage or as part of the post-incident activities.

78. William needs to validate his recovery efforts and intends to scan a web server he is responsible for with a scanning tool. What tool should he use to get the most useful information about system vulnerabilities?
    A. OpenVAS
    B. ZAP
    C. Wapiti
    D. Nmap

Answer: **A**

Explanation: OpenVAS is a full system vulnerability scanner.

79. What is the main objective of the containment phase of an incident response process?
    A. To restore systems to normal operation
    B. To prevent data exfiltration
    C. To limit further damage from occurring
    D. To limit leaks to the press or customers

Answer: **C**

Explanation: The containment stage of incident response is aimed at limiting damage and preventing any further damage from occurring. This may help stop data exfiltration, but the broader objective is to prevent all types of damage, including further exploits or compromises.

80. During an incident response process, Jane is assigned to gather details about what data was accessed, if it was exfiltrated and what type of data was exposed. Which of the following kind of analysis is she doing?
    A. Downtime Analysis
    B. Recovery Time Analysis
    C. Information Impact Analysis
    D. Economic Impact Analysis

Answer: **C**

Explanation: Jane is performing an information impact analysis. This involves determining what data was accessed if it was exfiltrated, and what impact that loss might have. An economic impact analysis looks at the financial impact of an event; downtime analysis reviews the time that services and systems will be down, and recovery time analysis estimates the time to return to service.

81. The incident response kit that Elizabeth is building is based around a powerful laptop so that she can execute on-site drive acquisitions and analysis. If she is expecting the need to acquire data from both SATA and IDE drives, which of the following item should she include in her kit?
    A. A USB hard drive
    B. A write blocker
    C. A USB-C cable
    D. A multi-interface drive adapter

Answer: **D**

Explanation: Elizabeth should ensure that she has at least one USB multi-interface drive adapter that can connect to both IDE and SATA drives.

82. Which of the following items is not typically found in corporate forensic kits?
    A. Crime Scene Tape
    B. Write Blockers

C. Decryption Tools
D. Label Makers

Answer: **A**

Explanation: Write blockers, label makers, and decryption tools are all commonly found in forensic kits used by both commercial and law enforcement staff. Crime scene tape is not a typical part of a forensic kit if you are not a law enforcement forensic analyst or officer. Some businesses may use seals or other indicators to discourage interference with investigations.

83. Which of the following administrations is not typically involved in post-incident communications?
A. Legal
B. Public Relations
C. Marketing
D. Developers

Answer: **D**

Explanation: Developers are typically not directly involved in post-incident communications, and are instead working to ensure the security of the applications or systems.

84. Elizabeth finds that the version of Java installed on her administration's web server has been replaced. Which of the following kind of issue is this best categorized as?
A. A Memory Overflow
B. Unexpected Input
C. An Unauthorized Change
D. Unauthorized Software

Answer: **C**

Explanation: Elizabeth's organization should use a change management process to avoid unauthorized changes to their web server. Elizabeth could then check the change process logs or audit trail to determine who made the change and when. If Java had been installed without proper authorization, then this would be unauthorized software. Unexpected input often occurs when web applications are attacked and may result in a memory overflow.

85. All of the following are considered intellectual property except for ________________.

   A. Trademarks
   B. Copyrights
   C. Patents
   D. Contracts

Answer: **D**

Explanation: Contracts are not considered intellectual property. Intellectual property includes the following:

   A. Patents
   B. Trade secrets
   C. Trademarks
   D. Copyrights
   E. Software Piracy and Licensing Issues
   F. Digital Rights Management (DRM)

86. Which of the following is *not* typically contained in a forensic kit?

   A. Polaroid Camera
   B. Removable Media
   C. Write Blocker
   D. Digital Forensics Workstation

Answer: **A**

Explanation: Digital SLR cameras, not Polaroid cameras, should be used for recording evidence.

87. Which of the following is the last phase in incident response?

   A. Recover
   B. Respond
   C. Report
   D. Review

Answer: **D**

Explanation: Steps in the incident response system can include the following:

A. Detect
B. Respond
C. Report
D. Recover
E. Remediate
F. Review

88. After examining the logs on the firewall, you discover that there is traffic leaving the network from one device on a regular schedule. Which of the following refers to traffic that leaves a network at regular intervals?

A. Beaconing
B. Exfiltration
C. Scan
D. Sweep

Answer: **A**

Explanation: Beaconing refers to traffic that leaves a network at regular intervals. This type of traffic could be generated by compromised hosts that are attempting to communicate with (or call home) the malicious party that compromised the host.

89. It has been brought to your attention that someone is using ICMP to gather information about the network. Which of the following uses ICMP to identify all live hosts?

A. Beaconing
B. Ping sweep
C. Port Scan
D. Vulnerability Scan

Answer: **B**

Explanation: Ping sweeps use ICMP to identify all live hosts by pinging all IP addresses in the known network. All devices that answer are up and running.

90. Which of the following roles must become involved only when a crime is discovered during a security incident?

A. Law Enforcement
B. Third-party Incident Response Providers
C. Technical
D. Management

Answer: **A**

Explanation: You are required to involve law enforcement only when a crime has been committed.

91. You are classifying the evidence you have collected from an incident. Which of the following symptoms would be considered a host-related symptom?
    A. Memory Overflows
    B. Unusual Network Traffic Spikes
    C. Beaconing
    D. Processor Consumption

Answer: **D**

Explanation: While processor consumption would be a host-related symptom, traffic spikes and beaconing are considered network symptoms, and memory overflows are an application-related symptom.

92. A user is frantic that his/her machine has been compromised. You are not convinced, but you continue to investigate the evidence. Which of the following is *not* a symptom of a compromised host?
    A. Scan Sweeps
    B. Processor Consumption
    C. Memory Consumption
    D. Drive Capacity Consumption

Answer: **A**

Explanation: Scan sweeps usually precede an attack but by themselves do not prove that a host is compromised.

93. After a new application is installed on an image that will be used in the Sales department, the application fails to function. You would like to examine the logs on the reference machine to see what may have gone wrong in the installation. What

type of Windows logs focuses on events that occur during the installation of a program?

A. Application
B. Setup
C. System
D. Security

Answer: **B**

Explanation: The Setup log focuses on events that occur during the installation of a program and useful for troubleshooting when an installation fails.

94. Which one of the following purposes are not one of the three main objectives that information security professionals must complete to protect their organizations against cybersecurity threats?

A. Confidentiality
B. Availability
C. Nonrepudiation
D. Integrity

Answer: **C**

Explanation: There are three main objectives of cybersecurity professionals, including confidentiality, integrity, and availability.

95. John is preparing to conduct a cybersecurity risk assessment for his organization. If he selects to follow the standard method proposed by NIST, which one of the following steps would come first?

A. Determine the impact
B. Determine the likelihood
C. Identify vulnerabilities
D. Identify threats

Answer: **D**

Explanation: The NIST risk assessment method says that organizations must identify threats before identifying vulnerabilities or defining the likelihood and impact of risks.

96. William completed a risk assessment and is determined that his network was vulnerable to hackers connecting to open ports on servers. He implemented a network firewall to reduce the likelihood of a successful attack. Which of the following risk management strategy did William choose to pursue?
    A. Risk Transference
    B. Risk Acceptance
    C. Risk Mitigation
    D. Risk Avoidance

Answer: **C**

Explanation: Any action that an organization takes to reduce the likelihood or impact of a risk is an example of risk mitigation.

97. Which of the following phase of a penetration test should the testers obtain written authorization to conduct during the test?
    A. Attack
    B. Planning
    C. Reporting
    D. Discovery

Answer: **B**

Explanation: The planning phase of a penetration test, the testers should confirm the timing, scope, and authorization for the test in writing.

98. Who is the best facilitator for a post-incident lessons-learned session?
    A. Independent Facilitator
    B. First Responder
    C. CEO
    D. CSIRT Leader

Answer: **A**

Explanation: Lessons-learned sessions are most effective when facilitated by an independent party who was not involved in the incident response effort.

99. John wants to use an active monitoring approach to test his network. Which of the

following methods is appropriate?

A. Enabling SNMP
B. Pinging remote systems
C. Using a protocol analyzer
D. Collecting NetFlow data

Answer: **B**

Explanation: Active monitoring is focused on reaching out to gather data using tools like ping and iPerf. Passive monitoring using protocol analyzers collects network traffic and router-based monitoring using SNMP, and flows gather data by receiving or collecting logged information.

100. Select one of the following that is not an Incident Management Process?

A. Preparation for Incident Response
B. Reporting
C. Detection and Analysis of Incident Response
D. Classification of an incident and its prioritization

Answer: **B**

Explanation: Reporting is not an incident management process. It is a responsibility of the Incident Response Team.

101. Select one from the following techniques in which a fake email that looks like an authentic email is sent to a target host.

A. Malware
B. Phishing
C. Social Engineering
D. Botnet

Answer: **B**

Explanation: Phishing process is a technique in which a fake email that looks like an authentic email is sent to a target host.

102. Which of the following flag does nmap use to enable operating system

identification?

A. -o
B. -osscan
C. -os
D. –id

Answer: **A**

Explanation: Nmap's operating system identification flag is –o. This enables OS detection. -A also enables OS identification and other features. –osscan with modifiers like –limit and –guess set specific OS identification features. –os and –id are not nmap flags.

103. Kim is deploying a new vulnerability scanner and wants to ensure the most accurate view of configuration issues on a computer system. The issues belong to traveling sales people. Which will be the best technology in this situation?

A. Server-based Scanning
B. Agent-based Scanning
C. Non-credentialed Scanning
D. Passive Network Monitoring

Answer: **B**

Explanation: By using an agent-based scanning approach, Kim will be provided with the most reliable results for systems that are not connected to the network. The scan can be run by the agent and the result is reported the next time the agent is connected to a network. It is required in all the technologies that the system is connected to the network during the scan.

104. During a port scan of a server, the following ports are discovered as open on the internal network by Miguel. The ports include TCP port 25, TCP port 80, TCP port 110, TCP port 443, TCP port 1433, TCP port 3389. The evidence of a variety of services running on this server is provided with this scan. Which one the following is *not an* indicated service by the scan results?

A. SSH
B. RDP
C. Web

D. Database

Answer: **B**

Explanation: Web servers are commonly allowed to be run on ports 80 (for HTTP) and 443 (for HTTPS). Database servers are allowed to be run ports 1433 (for Microsoft SQL Server), 1521 (for Oracle), or 3306 (for MySQL). Remote Desktop Protocol services are commonly allowed to be run on port 3389. The SSH using port 22 will not have any evidence of running on this server.

105. Beth is a software developer and the cybersecurity team of her company gives her a report of a vulnerability scan detecting an SQL injection vulnerability in one of her applications. She inspects her code and modify it in a test environment in order to correct the issues required to be corrected. What should be her next step?

A. Hire a consultant to perform a penetration test to confirm that the vulnerability is resolved
B. Mark the vulnerability as resolved and close the ticket
C. Request a scan of the test environment to confirm that the issue is corrected
D. Deploy the code to production immediately to resolve the vulnerability

Answer: **C**

Explanation: Beth should perform testing of her code before deploying it to production. Because this code was designed to correct an issue in a vulnerability scan, Beth should ask the security team to rerun the scan to confirm that the vulnerability scan was resolved as one component of her testing. A penetration test is overkilled and not necessary in this situation. Beth should not deploy the code to production until it is tested. She should not mark the issue as resolved until it is verified to work in production.

106. A port scan is run by a George on a network device. This port scanner is used by his organization. Which one of the following open ports represents the most important possible security vulnerability?

A. 22
B. 23
C. 161
D. 443

Answer: **B**

Explanation: Port 23 is used by telnet, an insecure unencrypted communication protocol. George should ensure that telnet is disabled and blocked. Secure shell (ssh) runs on port 22 and serves as a secure alternative. Port 161 is used by the Simple Network Management Protocol (SNMP), and port 443 is used for secure web connections.

107. In what type of attack, the other operating systems running in the same hardware environment are assigned with the adversary leveraging a position on a guest operating system to gain access to hardware resources?
   A. VM Escape
   B. Buffer Overflow
   C. Cross-site Scripting
   D. Directory Traversal

Answer: **A**

Explanation: In a VM escape attack, the vulnerabilities in the hypervisor are exploited by the attacker to gain access to resources assigned to other guest operating systems. Services running on the guest can be vulnerable to the other attacks listed in the question, but the other assigned resources would only be accessed by the attackers. These resources are assigned either to same guest, in the case of buffer overflow or directory traversal, or the client, in the case of cross-site scripting.

108. The presence of which of the following triggers specific vulnerability scanning requirements that is based upon law or regulation?
   A. Personally Identifiable Information
   B. Protected Health Information
   C. Credit Card Information
   D. Trade Secret Information

Answer: **C**

Explanation: While the vulnerability scanning should be triggered by all of these categories of information for assets involved in their processing, storage, or transmission, only credit card information has specific regulations covering these scans. The detailed requirements for vulnerability scanning are contained in The Payment Card Industry Data Security Standard (PCI DSS).

109. For a large network of sensors, Harry developed a vulnerability scanning program. The sensors are used by his organization to monitor a transcontinental gas pipeline. What term is used to describe this type of sensor network commonly?

A. WLAN
B. VPN
C. P2P
D. SCADA

Answer: **D**

Explanation: SCADA, Supervisory Control and Data Acquisition, network is a form of industrial control system (ICS). This network is used to maintain control systems and sensors over a geographic area that is very large.

110. A vulnerability scan is run by Eric in an attempt to detect a vulnerability that was announced by a software manufacturer the day before. In spite of having the issues with at least two of his servers, the scanner could not detect the vulnerability. Then Eric contacted the vulnerability scanning vendor who assured him of the release of a signature for the vulnerability overnight. What should be the next step taken by Eric?

A. Check the affected servers to verify a false positive
B. Check the affected servers to verify a false negative
C. Report a bug to the vendor
D. Update the vulnerability signatures

Answer: **D**

Explanation: The most recent signatures from the vendor's vulnerability feed has not been pulled by the Eric's scanner that is most likely issue being faced. A manual update should be performed by Eric and the scan is rerun before performing an investigation of the servers in question or filing a bug report.

111. A vulnerability scan of a web application was run by Natalie. The web application was deployed by her organization. As the result of this scan, a blind SQL injection

was reported. She then reported the vulnerability to the developers who made a few modifications but any evidence of this possible attack was not visible to her. She ran the scan and the same result was received. The code is now being insisted as secured by the developers. What could be the result generated from the above assumption?

A. The result is a false positive
B. The code is deficient and requires correction
C. The vulnerability is in a different web application running on the same server
D. Natalie is misreading the scan report

Answer: **A**

Explanation: It is very difficult to detect a Blind SQL injection vulnerabilities. These vulnerabilities are a notorious source of false positive reports. The results of the tests performed by the developers should be verified by Natalie. It should be very open to the possibility that this is a false positive report, since it is the most likely scenario.

112. A missing Windows security patch was discovered by the Frank. The patch arose during a vulnerability scan of a server in his organization's data center. The system was discovered to be virtualized upon further investigation. Where could be the patch applied?

A. To the virtualized system
B. To the domain controller
C. To the virtualization platform
D. The patch is not necessary

Answer: **A**

Explanation: The full versions of operating systems are being run by Virtualized systems. If a missing operating system patch is revealed by Frank's scan while scanning a virtualized server, that guest operating system should directly be applied with the patch.

113. The high level of false positive reports that are produced by the vulnerability scans is making Andrew upset. The series of actions are then designed considerably to reduce the false positive rate. The desired effect is then considered to be *least* likely residing in which one of the following?

A. Moving to credentialed scanning

B. Moving to agent-based scanning
C. Integrating asset information into the scan
D. Increasing the sensitivity of scans

Answer: **D**

Explanation: The quality and quantity of information available to the scanner can be improved by Andrew as he moves to credentialed scanning, agent-based scanning, and the asset information is integrated into the scans. The false positive rate is then likely to be reduced by any of these actions, which are likely to reduce the false positive rate. The increased sensitivity scans would likely have the opposite effect that allows even more false positives to be reported by the scanner.

114. The vulnerability management program of an organization is being upgraded by Laura. The system's configuration recovering technology is being added by her in spite of being highly secured. Local authentication is used by many of the systems, and the burden of maintaining accounts on all of those systems is desired to be avoided. In order to meet the requirements, what technology should Laura consider using?

A. Credentialed Scanning
B. Un-credentialed Scanning
C. Server-based Scanning
D. Agent-based Scanning

Answer: **D**

Explanation: The deployment of the vulnerability scanning agents on the servers, that needs to be scanned, is taken under consideration by Laura. The configuration information is then retrieved by these agents and sent to the scanner for analysis. This information could also be retrieved by credentialed scanning but on each scanned system, accounts are required to be managed by Laura. In Server-based Scanning, the configuration information cannot be retrieved from the host unless run in credentialed mode. While in noncredentialed Scans, the detailed configuration information from scan targets is not retrieved.

115. Referring a SQL injection exploit, an access to a database is typically gained by exploiting a vulnerability in which one of the following?

A. Operating System

B. Web Application
C. Database Server
D. Firewall

Answer: **B**

Explanation: The data stored in enterprise databases is targeted by the SQL injection vulnerabilities but this is done by exploiting flaws in client-facing applications. These flaws are not exclusively found but are most common in web applications.

116. The theft of sensitive information stored in a database is taken under consideration by Gene. The most direct threat to this information is posed by which one of the following vulnerabilities?
A. SQL Injection
B. Cross-site Scripting
C. Buffer Overflow
D. Denial of Service

Answer: **A**

Explanation: An information stored in the database has a theoretical impact of a buffer overflow attack, a more direct threat is posed by a SQL injection that allows an attacker to execute arbitrary SQL commands on the database server. In Cross-site scripting attacks, the database access is not allowed as they are primarily user-based threats. In a denial-of-service attack, the system availability is targeted rather than information disclosure.

117. An old vulnerability scanner is restarted by Morgan that had not been used in more than a year. The scanner was booted, logged in, and configured to run a scan. The result found showed that the known vulnerabilities were not found being detected by the scanner as were detected by other scanners. What could be the main cause for this issue?
A. The scanner is running on an outdated operating system
B. The scanner's maintenance subscription has expired
C. Morgan has invalid credentials on the scanner
D. The scanner does not have a current, valid IP address

Answer: **B**

Explanation: While the scanner was inactive and is not able to retrieve current signatures from the vendor's vulnerability feed, the maintenance subscription for the scanner expired that is the most likely issue. The scan results should not be affected by the operating system of the scanner. The scanner having an invalid IP address or invalid credentials could not be accessed by Morgan.

118. Both internal and external vulnerability scans of a web server is run by Carla and a possible SQL injection vulnerability is being detected. The vulnerability does not appear in the external scan but only appears in the internal scan. The requests coming from the internal scan and some from the external scanner can be seen when Carla checks the server logs but no evidence that a SQL injection exploit was attempted by the external scanner. For these results, what is the most likely explanation?

A. A host firewall is blocking external network connections to the web server
B. A network firewall is blocking external network connections to the web server
C. A host IPS is blocking some requests to the web server
D. A network IPS is blocking some requests to the web server

Answer: **D**

Explanation: SQL injection attempts are sent to the server blocked by a network. IPS is the most likely scenario for this question. On the network, the internal scanner is positioned in such a way that it is not filtered by the network IPS. If the requests were being blocked by a host IPS the vulnerability would not appear on internal scans either. No external scanner entries would appear in the log file if the requests were being blocked by the firewall.

119. A vulnerability scanning workflow is designed by Carla. She has been tasked with selecting a responsible person for remediating vulnerabilities. To remediate a server vulnerability, which one of the following people would normally be in the *best* position?

A. Cybersecurity Analyst
B. System Administrator
C. Network Engineer
D. IT Manager

Answer: **B**

Explanation: To remediate the vulnerabilities, system engineers are normally in the best position since they are responsible for maintaining the server configuration. An input may be provided by the network engineers, security analysts, and managers but they often lack either the privileges or knowledge to remediate a server successfully.

120. A web server running on a network is discovered to be having access to a database server that should be restricted while Edward was performing a vulnerability scan. Both the servers are running on the VMware virtualization platform of the organization. To configure a security control in order to restrict this access, where should Edward look?
    A. VMware
    B. Data Center Firewall
    C. Perimeter (Internet) Firewall
    D. Intrusion Prevention System

Answer: **A**

Explanation: The network traffic never leaves that environment of having both of the hosts located on the same virtualization platform. Since both of these hosts are located on the same virtualization platform and the network traffic never leaves that environment, the network traffic would not be controlled by an intrusion prevention system or an external network firewall. The internal configuration of the virtual network should be considered by Edward in order to determine whether they can apply the restrictions there.

121. A vulnerability scanner that will run scans of a network is being configured by Renee. The use of a daily vulnerability scans is the requirement of corporate policy. What could be the best time to configure the scans?
    A. During the day, when operations reach their peak to stress test systems
    B. During the evening, when operations are minimal to reduce the impact on systems
    C. During lunch hour, when people have stepped away from their systems but there is still considerable load
    D. On the weekends, when the scans may run unimpeded

Answer: **B**

Explanation: As per accordance to the corporate policy, the scans must be run by Renee on a daily basis, hence the weekend is not a viable option. The scan should be carried out at a time when they have the least impact on operations, which would be in the evening time in this scenario. The identification of the known vulnerabilities in systems is the main purpose of the vulnerability scan, not the load testing of servers.

122. A vulnerability scan is run by Terry against his organization's credit card processing environment and a number of vulnerabilities was found. In order to have a "clean" scan under PCI DSS standards, which of the following vulnerabilities must he remediate?

A. Critical Vulnerabilities
B. Critical and High Vulnerabilities
C. Critical, High, and Moderate Vulnerabilities
D. Critical, High, Moderate, and Low Vulnerabilities

Answer: **B**

Explanation: It is required in the PCI DSS standard that a clean scan result showing no critical or high vulnerabilities in order to maintain compliance is presented by the merchants and service providers.

123. A configuration management agent was discovered by Patrick during a vulnerability scan. This agent is installed on all of his organization's Windows servers that contain a serious vulnerability. A patch is available for this as the manufacturer is aware of the issue. In order to correct this issue, what process should Patrick follow?

A. Immediately deploy the patch to all affected systems
B. Deploy the patch to a single production server for testing and then deploy to all servers if that test is successful
C. Deploy the patch in a test environment and then conduct a staged roll-out in production
D. Disable all external access to systems until the patch is deployed

Answer: **C**

Explanation: The patch, that is described in the question, should be handled with extreme care by Patrick. If any of the services fails due to this patch, all of the Windows servers of the organization could be potentially disabled as a result. This is a serious risk and a testing is required before deploying a patch. The best course of action of Patrick is to deploy the patch in a test environment and then it is rolled out into production on a staged basis when the test is successful. Options involving the deployment of the patch to production systems before testing may result in failure of services. It is an overreaction to disable all external access to systems that would have critical business impact.

124. When prioritizing the remediation of vulnerabilities, which one of the following is not an appropriate criteria to use?

A. Network exposure of the affected system
B. Difficulty of remediation
C. Severity of the vulnerability
D. All of these are appropriate

Answer: **D**

Explanation: When prioritizing remediation of vulnerabilities, all of the factors given in the question should be considered by a cybersecurity analyst. The severity of the vulnerability increases with increasing the risk involved in it. The chances of the vulnerability being exploited may be increased or reduced based upon the network exposure of the affected system. The ability of team to correct the issue with a reasonable commitment of resources may get impacted by the difficulty of remediation.

125. A vulnerability scan of a dedicated Apache server is run by Landon that is planned to be moved into a DMZ of his organization. The informative results are the *least* likely to be provided by which one of the following vulnerability scans?

A. Web Application Vulnerability Scan
B. Database Vulnerability Scan
C. Port Scan
D. Network Vulnerability Scan

Answer: **B**

Explanation: The given scenario shows no indication of the server running a database; Actually, it is indicated in the scenario that the server is dedicated to running the Apache web service. Therefore, it is unlikely that any results are yielded by a database vulnerability scan. The other three scans should be run by Landon and a specialized database vulnerability scan could be followed up if the presence of a database server is indicated.

126. The cybersecurity vulnerability management program is run by Ted for his organization. A database administrator is being sent a report of a missing database patch that corrects a high severity security issue. Ted then gets a written statement by DBA that the patch has been applied. When Ted reruns the scan, the same vulnerability is being reported again. What should be the next step taken by Ted?

A. Mark the vulnerability as a false positive
B. Ask the DBA to recheck the database
C. Mark the vulnerability as an exception
D. Escalate the issue to the DBA's manager

Answer: **B**

Explanation: The DBA is asked to recheck the server by Ted, in this case, to ensure that the patch was properly applied. The issue is not marked as an appropriate false positive report until a brief investigation is performed by Ted to confirm that the patch is applied properly. This is true since the vulnerability relates to a missing patch that is not a common source of false positive reports. Ted should not mark it as an exception as there was no acceptance of this vulnerability. Since the DBA is working with him in good faith, this issue should not be escalated to management by Ted.

127. A vulnerability scan is being conducted by Ben for a new client of his security consulting organization. Which one from the following steps is performed first?

A. Conducting penetration testing
B. Running a vulnerability evaluation scan
C. Running a discovery scan
D. Obtaining permission for the scans

Answer: **D**

Explanation: Ben should take permission to perform scans from the client before getting engaged in any other activities. The laws may be violated as a result of any failure and/or the client may get angry.

128. The remediation of security vulnerabilities is being coordinated in an organization and Katherine is trying to work with a system engineer on the patching of a server to correct a vulnerability of a moderate impact. The server patching is refused by the engineer as a critical business process running on the server gets a potential interruption. Which course of the action is the most

reasonable for Katherine to be taken?

A. Schedule the patching to occur during a regular maintenance cycle
B. Exempt the server from patching because of the critical business impact
C. Demand that the server be patched immediately to correct the vulnerability
D. Inform the engineer that if he does not apply the patch within a week, Katherine will file a complaint to his manager

Answer: **A**

Explanation: The importance of the patch increases due to the fact that a critical business process is run by the server, rather than deferring it indefinitely. The occurrence of the patch during a regular maintenance window is scheduled as Katherine working with the engineer. Since it has a relatively low impact of the vulnerability, waiting for it is reasonable until the window is scheduled.

129. The most current and accurate information about the presence of vulnerabilities arising due to the misconfiguration of operating system settings is provided by which one of the following approaches?

A. On-demand Vulnerability Scanning
B. Continuous Vulnerability Scanning
C. Scheduled Vulnerability Scanning
D. Agent-based Monitoring

Answer: **D**

Explanation: A vulnerability scans provides a snapshot in time of a security status of the system from the perspective of the vulnerability scanner. A detailed view of the system's configuration is provided by an agent-based monitoring from an internal perspective and more accurate results are likely to be provided, regardless of the vulnerability scanning frequency.

130. The vulnerability scanning for a new web server is being configured by Garrett. The web server is being deployed on a DMZ network of the organization. The public website if a company is hosted by the server. For getting the best results, what type of scanning should Garrett configure?

A. Garrett should not perform scanning of DMZ systems
B. Garrett should perform external scanning only
C. Garrett should perform internal scanning only

D. Garrett should perform both internal and external scanning

Answer: **D**

Explanation: Garret should combine both internal and external vulnerability scans in order to get the best results. An "attacker's eye view" of the web server is provided with the external scan while the exploitable vulnerabilities, which are to be exploited by an insider or an attacker who has gained access to another system on the network, are uncovered by the internal scans.

131. The vulnerability scans of a dedicated network are being configured by James. These networks are being used for processing credit card transactions. What are the important scan types to be included in the scanning program of James?

A. Scans from a dedicated scanner on the card processing network
B. Scans from an external scanner on his organization's network
C. Scans from an external scanner operated by an approved scanning vendor
D. All three types of scans are equally important

Answer: **D**

Explanation: James is provided with important information using all three of these scan types and/or the regulatory requirements need to be met with these scan types. The information on services accessible outside of the payment card network is provided by the external scan from James' own network. The vulnerabilities that are accessible to an insider or someone who has breached the network perimeter and is detected by the internal scan. To meet the PCI DSS obligations, the Approved Scanning Vendor (ASV) scans are required. The same level of detailed reporting is not normally provided while running ASV scans infrequently. The scan is run by the organization's own external scans. Hence, James should include all three types of scan in his program.

132. A vulnerability scan of a network was run by Ted and was overwhelmed with results. The most important vulnerabilities were to be focused. What could be the strategy taken by Ted to reconfigure his vulnerability scanner?

A. Increase the scan sensitivity
B. Decrease the scan sensitivity
C. Increase the scan frequency
D. Decrease the scan frequency

Answer: **B**

Explanation: As Ted decreases the scan sensitivity, the number of results returned by the scan can be reduced. In this way the threshold for reporting will be increased and will only return the most important results. While increasing the scan, sensitivity would have the opposite effect that results in increasing the number of reported vulnerabilities. The number of reported vulnerabilities would not be altered by changing the scan frequency.

133. In a virtualization platform, which one of the following protocols might be used for monitoring and management of the network?

A. SNMP
B. SMTP
C. BGP
D. EIGRP

Answer: **A**

Explanation: Traps and polling requests are used by the Simple Network Management Protocol (SNMP). This protocol is used to monitor and manage both physical and virtual networks. The Simple Mail Transfer Protocol, SMTP, is an email transfer protocol. The routing decisions are made by using the Border Gateway Protocol (BGP) and Enhanced Interior Gateway Routing Protocol (EIGRP)

134. Bring your own device or BYOD policy is being implemented for mobile devices by Tom's company. The secure use of sensitive information on personally owned devices besides providing administrators with the ability to wipe corporate information from the device without affecting personal data is allowed by which one of the following technologies?

A. Remote Wipe
B. Strong Passwords
C. Biometric Authentication
D. Containerization

Answer: **D**

Explanation: The security of mobile devices shares the contribution for all of the technologies listed in the question. The isolation is allowed only with containerization. Also, it allows protection of sensitive information separately from other uses of the device. A secure vault for corporate information is created by the Containerization technology that may be wiped remotely without affecting other uses of the device. The contents of the container are also protected from other applications and services running on the device.

135. A system with a high priority vulnerability management was discovered during a vulnerability scan. Sally requires to patch this vulnerability. The system is located behind a firewall and no imminent threat is present but Sally wants to get the situation resolved as quickly as possible. What would be the best course of action taken by her?

A. Initiating a high-priority change through her organization's change management process
B. Implementing a fix immediately and then documenting the change after the fact
C. Implementing a fix immediately and then informing her supervisor of her action and the rationale
D. Scheduling a change for the next quarterly patch cycle

Answer: **A**

Explanation: Any of the imminent threat is not recognized by Sally in this situation. Therefore, an emergency change process is not necessarily followed. This emergency change process would allow her to implement the change before conducting any change management. It is said that the change should be made for a scheduled patch cycle, without waiting up to three months. Hence, the best option of Sally is to initiate a high-priority change through the change management process of her organization.

136. A PCI DSS vulnerability scan of a web server was conducted by Veronica and a critical PHP vulnerability requiring an upgrade to correct was noted. The update was then applied. How soon will the scan be repeated by Veronica?

A. Within 30 days
B. At the next scheduled quarterly scan
C. At the next scheduled annual scan
D. Immediately

Answer: **D**

Explanation: It is required to rerun the vulnerability scan. Veronica runs this scan until she receives a clear result. This result may be submitted for PCI DSS compliance purposes.

137. The security of an industrial control system is given an attention in an organization of Bruce. This control system is used to monitor and manage systems in their factories. The risk of an attacker penetrating this system needs to be reduced. The vulnerabilities in this type of system would be mitigated by which one of the following security controls?

A. Network Segmentation
B. Input Validation
C. Memory Protection
D. Redundancy

Answer: **A**

Explanation: One of the strongest controls is Network Segmentation. These controls may be used to protect industrial control systems and SCADA systems. They are controlled by isolating them from other systems on the network. Some security may be provided by input validation and memory protection. Isolating these sensitive systems from other devices and preventing an attacker from connecting to them in the first place is not as strong as the mitigating effect. The uptime from accidental failures is increased by Redundancy but the systems would not be protected from the attack.

138. An administrative interface to one of the storage systems of Frank that was discovered during a vulnerability scan was inadvertently exposed to the internet. The firewall logs are reviewed and also determined whether any access attempts came from external sources. By which one of the following IP addresses an external source is reflected?

A. 10.15.1.100
B. 12.8.1.100
C. 172.16.1.100
D. 192.168.1.100

Answer: **B**

Explanation: Private IP addresses are the addresses in the 10.x.x.x, 172.16.x.x, and 192.168.x.x ranges. These IP addresses are not routable over the Internet. Therefore, out of the addresses listed in the question, only 12.8.1.100 could originate outside the local network.

139. The vulnerability scans for a Nick's network is configured by using a third-party vulnerability scanning service. A web server exposing a CIFS file share and containing several significant vulnerabilities needs to be scanned. Only the ports 80 and 443 are shown as open in the scan results. What could be the most likely cause of these scan results?

A. The CIFS file share is running on port 443
B. A firewall configuration is preventing the scan from succeeding
C. The scanner configuration is preventing the scan from succeeding
D. The CIFS file share is running on port 80

Answer: **B**

Explanation: Between the server and the third-party scanning service, there is a network firewall that is the most likely issue here. The inbound connections to the web server are being blocked by this firewall and also the external scan is prevented from succeeding. Port 445 generally allows running CIFS and not port 80 or 443. Web services are commonly associated with these ports. The other ports on the server are being detected by scanner successfully and is not likely misconfigured. The firewall rules should either be altered to allow the scan to succeed or place a scanner on a network preferably by Nick in closer proximity to the web server.

140. A vulnerability scan of all servers in the organization's data center of Brian is configured. The highest-severity vulnerabilities are detected by configuring the scan. System administrators are empowered to correct issues on the servers of an organization. Also, there must be some understanding of the status of those remediation. The interests of the Brian would be best served by which one of the following?

A. Giving the administrators access to view the scans in the vulnerability scanning system
B. Sending email alerts to administrators when the scans detect a new vulnerability on their servers
C. Configuring the vulnerability scanner to open a trouble ticket when they detect a new vulnerability on a server

D. Configuring the scanner to send reports to Brian who can notify administrators

Answer: **C**

Explanation: The existing trouble ticket system of the organization is the most leveraged path to be followed by Brian. This system is likely used by the administrator on a regular basis, and reporting and escalation of issues can be handled by it. The scanner may be given an administrator access and/or may send the emailed reports automatically, but those will not provide the tracking that he desires.

141. A new vulnerability scanner is being configured for use in the organization's data center of Tonya. For the update frequency of scanner, which one of the following values is considered a best practice?

A. Daily
B. Weekly
C. Monthly
D. Quarterly

Answer: **A**

Explanation: Vulnerability scanners needs to be updated as often as possible in order to allow the scanner to retrieve new vulnerability signatures as soon as they are released. Tonya must choose the daily updates.

142. The success of the vulnerability management program is evaluated and needs some matrices to be included by Don. Which would be the *least* useful metric from the following?

A. Time to resolve critical vulnerabilities
B. Number of open critical vulnerabilities over time
C. Total number of vulnerabilities reported
D. Number of systems containing critical vulnerabilities

Answer: **C**

Explanation: The high-priority vulnerabilities should likely be the main focus of Don's efforts as results for almost any scanned system will be reported by a vulnerability scanner. The useful metrics includes the number of open critical vulnerabilities over time, the time to resolve critical vulnerabilities, and the number of systems containing critical vulnerabilities. Any severity information is not included in the total number of reported vulnerabilities hence it is less useful.

143. A vulnerability scan of a network of a client is being run by Dave for the first time. This type of scan has never been run by Dave who expects to find many results. The largest portion of the vulnerabilities discovered in Dave's scan is likely to be remediated by which security control?

A. Input Validation
B. Patching
C. Intrusion Prevention Systems
D. Encryption

Answer: **B**

Explanation: Some of the vulnerabilities that were discovered by Dave's scan may be remediated by all of the listed solutions. The missing security updates results in the vast majority of issues in an unmaintained network. Quite a few vulnerabilities are being resolved by applying patches.

144. The network of the Matt's organization is being integrated with that of a recently acquired company. The main concerned of the company is that, the acquired company's network contains systems with exploitable vulnerabilities and the network needs to be protected against compromised hosts on the new network. In order to reduce the risk from network interconnection, which one of the following controls would be the *least* effective?

A. Network Segmentation
B. VLAN Separation
C. Firewall
D. Proxy Server

Answer: **D**

Explanation: The two networks should be separated using a network segmentation technique, in doing so Matt places the new company on a separate VLAN. It would not be effective to use a proxy server because there is no indication that the either of the networks intend to offer services to the other.

145. A production system is being patched by Rhonda to correct a detected vulnerability during a scan. In order to minimize the risk of a system failure, what process should she follow?

A. Rhonda should deploy the patch immediately on the production system
B. Rhonda should wait 60 days to deploy the patch to determine whether bugs are reported
C. Rhonda should deploy the patch in a sandbox environment to test it prior to applying it in production
D. Rhonda should contact the vendor to determine a safe timeframe for deploying the patch in production

Answer: **C**

Explanation: The patch should be deployed in a sandbox environment and then tested thoroughly prior to releasing it in production. In this way, Rhonda reduces the risk that the patch will not work well in her environment. Some of the issues may be identified simply by asking the vendor or waiting for 60 days but the risk is not sufficiently reduced by this because in her company's environment, the patch will not have been tested.

146. In the case where no other information is given, which one of the following vulnerabilities will be considered as the greatest threat to information confidentiality?

A. HTTP TRACE/TRACK methods enabled
B. SSL Server with SSLv3 enabled vulnerability
C. phpinfo information disclosure vulnerability
D. Web application SQL injection vulnerability

Answer: **D**

Explanation: A confidentiality risk is posed by all of these vulnerabilities, the greatest threat is posed by the SQL injection vulnerability since the contents of a backend database is allowed to be retrieved by an attacker. The reconnaissance information may be provided by The HTTP TRACK/TRACE methods and PHP information disclosure vulnerabilities but the sensitive information would not be directly disclosed. SSLv3 is no longer considered as secure rather it is much more difficult to exploit for information theft than a SQL injection issue.

147. The system in the organization that is subjected to vulnerability scanning is being determined by Mary. This decision is taken on the base of the criticality of the system to business operations. To find the information, where should Mary turn to?

A. The CEO
B. System Names
C. IP Addresses
D. Asset Inventory

Answer: **D**

Explanation: The asset inventory of an organization should be consulted by Mary. The information about asset criticality should resides in this inventory if it is constructed and maintained properly. The CEO may be aware of some of this information but there is no chance that he or she would have all of the necessary information or the time to review it. Some hints may reside in system names and IP addresses to asset criticality but would not be as good a source as an asset inventory that clearly identifies criticality.

148. A vulnerability management system for the organization is being designed by Amy. The conservation of a network bandwidth is her highest priority. The configuration or applications installed on target systems could not be altered. In Amy's environment, what would be the best solution to provide vulnerability reports?

A. Agent-based Scanning
B. Server-based Scanning
C. Passive Network Monitoring
D. Port Scanning

Answer: **C**

Explanation: Amy's requirements to minimize network bandwidth consumption is met by passive network monitoring. The installation of an agent is not required in passive network monitoring. The agent-based scanning requires application installation, hence cannot be used by Amy. Also, the server-based scanning consumes bandwidth thus, she should not use it. The vulnerability reports are not provided with port scanning.

149. A vendor security bulletin describing a zero-day vulnerability is received by Laura in her organization's main database server. This server is used by publicly accessible web applications and is on a private network. The decryption of administrative connections to the server is allowed by the vulnerability. What could be the reasonable action that Laura can take to address this issue as quickly as possible?

A. Apply a vendor patch that resolves the issue
B. Disable all administrative access to the database server
C. Require VPN access for remote connections to the database server
D. Verify that the web applications use strong encryption

Answer: **C**

Explanation: The possibility of eavesdropping on administrative connections to the database server is the issue raised by this vulnerability. The strong encryption to this connection described in the question would be added by the use of a VPN and the effect of the vulnerability is negated. It would be unnecessarily disruptive to the business to disable an administrative access to the database server. To the issue, the web server's encryption level is irrelevant as the connections to the web server, and not the database server, would be affected by it.

150. A vulnerability scanning tool is being configured by Beth. She learned about a privilege escalation vulnerability recently that requires the user to have local access to the system. Beth is ensuring that this vulnerability, as well as future similar vulnerabilities, are being detected. In order to improve the scanner's ability to detect this type of issue, what action can she take?

A. Enable credentialed scanning
B. Run a manual vulnerability feed update
C. Increase scanning frequency
D. Change the organization's risk appetite

Answer: **A**

Explanation: The likelihood of detecting vulnerabilities requiring local access to a server would be increased by enabling credentialed scanning. The deep configuration settings that might not be available with a non-credentialed scan of a properly secured system can be read by credentialed scans. A signature for this particular vulnerability may be added by updating the vulnerability feed manually but with future vulnerabilities, it would not get any assistance and Beth should configure automatic feed updates instead. The speed of detection is increased by increasing the scanning frequency but the scanner's ability to detect the vulnerability would not be impacted by it. The selection of the vulnerabilities to be accepted by an organization would be affected by the organization's risk appetite but the ability of the scanner to detect a vulnerability would not be changed.

151. The vulnerability scan report for a web server was reviewed and the multiple SQL injection and cross-site scripting vulnerabilities were found in the report. Shannon reviewed this vulnerability scan report. What would be the least difficult way for Shannon to address these issues?

A. Installing a web application firewall
B. Recoding the web application to include input validation
C. Applying security patches to the server operating system
D. Applying security patches to the web server service

Answer: **A**

Explanation: The SQL injection or cross-site scripting flaws will not be corrected just by applying patches to the server since these flaws resides within the web applications themselves. Applying patches to the server will not correct SQL injections or cross-site scripting flaws, as these reside within the web applications themselves. The root cause could be corrected as Shannon recodes the web applications to use input validation but this path is more difficult. The immediate protection with lower effort would be provided by a web application firewall.

152. Which one of the following is the most difficult vulnerability to confirm with an external vulnerability scan?

A. Cross-site Scripting
B. Cross-site Request Forgery
C. Blind SQL Injection
D. Unpatched Web Server

Answer: **C**

Explanation: The easy to detect vulnerabilities are cross-site scripting and cross-site request forgery. These vulnerabilities can be detected with vulnerability scans since the visual confirmation of a successful attack can be obtained by the scanner. The publicly accessible banner information is often used to identify the unpatched web servers. In spite of the fact that the scanners can often detect many types of SQL injection vulnerabilities, the confirmation of the blind SQL injection vulnerabilities is often very difficult as the results to the attacker rely upon the silent (blind) execution of code.

153. The ability of Ann's organization to detect and remediate security vulnerabilities is likely be improved by adopting a continuous monitoring approach. From the following options given, which one is *not* a characteristic of a continuous monitoring program?

A. Analyzing and reporting findings
B. Conducting forensic investigations when a vulnerability is exploited
C. Mitigating the risk associated with findings
D. Transferring the risk associated with a finding to a third party

Answer: **B**

Explanation: It is one of the core tasks of a continuous monitoring program to analyze and report findings to management. Responding to findings by mitigating, transferring, accepting, or avoiding risks would be another core task. As continuous monitoring programs are an incident response process, they are not tasked with performing forensic investigations.

154. Configuration changes to a vulnerability scanner are being reported immediately by using which one of the following strategies?

A. Scheduled Scans
B. Continuous Monitoring
C. Automated Remediation
D. Automatic Updates

Answer: **B**

Explanation: The agents installed on monitored systems are used in continuous monitoring to report the configuration changes to the vulnerability scanner immediately. Any of the changes would not be detected by scheduled scans until they are run the next time. The security issues rather than the report configuration changes would be corrected by the automated remediation. The scans using the most current vulnerability information would be ensured by automatic updates.

155. A vulnerability management program for a company is being implemented while Norman works with his manager. The remediation of critical and high-severity risks should be of main focus as his manager suggested him and no time should be wasted worrying about risks rated medium or lower. What could be the criteria that Norman's manager should use to make this decision?

A. Risk Appetite
B. False Positive
C. False Negative
D. Data Classification

Answer: **A**

Explanation: The organization's risk appetite (or risk tolerance) in order to make a decision has been decided to be used by Norman's manager. The medium severity risks will not be tolerated and the critical or high-severity risks will not be accepted by the organization as per his statement. As the specific vulnerabilities are not being discussed, this is not a case of a false positive or false negative error. The criticality or sensitivity of information was also not discussed; thus the decision is not based upon data classification.

156. An operating system vulnerability on a system on Laura's network was discovered. The vulnerability on a search appliance installed on her network was also discovered after tracing the IP address. She was informed that the underlying operating system has no access when consulted with the responsible engineer. What is the best course of action for Laura?

A. Contact the vendor to obtain a patch
B. Try to gain access to the underlying operating system and install the patch
C. Mark the vulnerability as a false positive
D. Wait 30 days and rerun the scan to see whether the vendor corrected the vulnerability

Answer: **A**

Explanation: A vendor should be contacted by Laura in order to determine whether a patch is available for the appliance. The appliance should not be modified as it may result in operational issues. Laura should contact the vendor to determine whether a patch is available for the appliance. She should not attempt to modify the appliance herself, as this may cause operational issues. Laura has no evidence to indicate that this is a false positive report and waiting 30 days to see whether the problem resolves itself does not sound sensible.

157. In the United States, which one of the following types of data is subjected to regulations to specify the minimum frequency of vulnerability scanning?

A. Driver's License Numbers
B. Insurance Records
C. Credit Card Data
D. Medical Records

Answer: **C**

Explanation: Credit card information is subject to the Payment Card Industry Data Security Standard (PCI DSS), the specific provisions dictating the frequency of vulnerability scanning resides in it. The other data types mentioned in the question are regulated instead and the specific provisions that identify a required vulnerability scanning frequency resides in none of those regulations.

158. A password policy is being designed for Roberta's organization. The length of exposure of an account with a compromised password is intended to be limited by including a control. Roberta's goal would be met by which one of the following controls?

A. Minimum Password Length
B. Password History
C. Password Expiration
D. Password Complexity

Answer: **C**

Explanation: Password expiration policy is the primary control used to limit the length of exposure of compromised passwords. A password change would be forced at a defined interval in this policy and either the intruder would be locked out (if the legitimate user changes the password) or the legitimate user would be given an alert to the compromise (if the intruder changes the password).

159. A multifactor authentication is implemented for Angela's organization and she has been offered a number of choices. Which one of the following choices is not an example of multifactor authentication?

A. Password and Retina Scan
B. PIN and SMS Token
C. Password and Security Questions
D. Password and SMS Token

Answer: **C**

Explanation: The password and security questions option should not be selected as they both are both examples of knowledge-based factors. Different factors providing a greater level of security are included in each of the other answers.

160. A database server that will provide analytics support to a data science team within Allan's organization is being built. Given below is the current layout of his organization's network. For this server, which network zone would be the most appropriate?

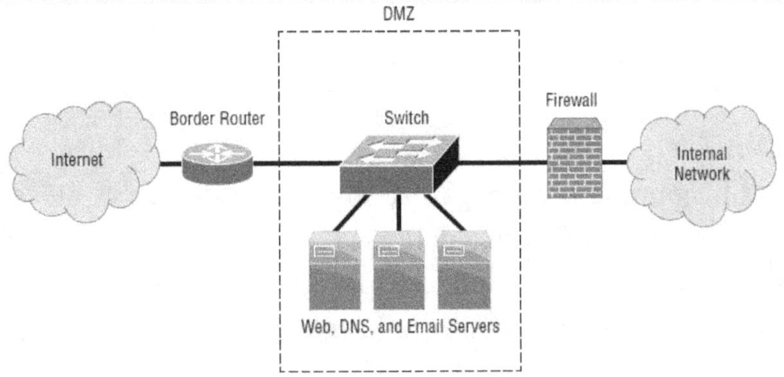

A. Internet
B. Internal Network
C. DMZ
D. New Network Connected to the Firewall

Answer: **B**

Explanation: The most appropriate zone for this server is the internal network, as only the internal clients on the data science team is being served. It is very costly to add an additional network for this server and no indications are there that the effort and expense would be justified. A database server should never be placed on the Internet, and there is no requirement of public access, which would justify placing it in the DMZ.

161. Ursula wants to use a dual firewall approach and is considering to redesign her network, as shown here. Over a triple homed firewall, which one of the following is an advantage of this approach?

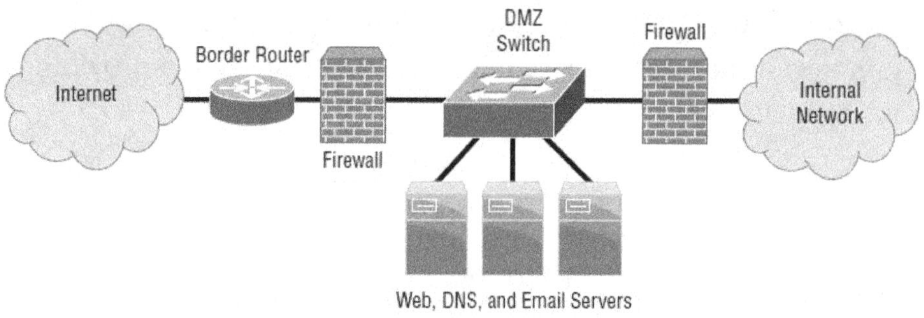

A. Increased Redundancy
B. Decreased Cost
C. Hardware Diversity
D. Simplified Administration

Answer: **C**

Explanation: With a dual firewall approach, an organization is allowed to achieve hardware diversity by using firewalls from different vendors. Rather than decreasing, this approach typically increases both the cost and complexity of administration. Proposed design would not be indicated as to increase redundancy over the existing environment.

162. Select one from the following security activities that is not a component of the operations and the SDLC's maintenance phase.

A. Vulnerability Scans
B. Disposition
C. Patching
D. Regression Testing

Answer: **B**

Explanation: A separate SDLC phase is Disposition. In its design, it is ensured that the data is properly purged at the end of an application life cycle. The ongoing vulnerability scans, patching, and regression testing after upgrades are included in operations and maintenance activities.

163. The procedures of John's organization are being reviewed for applying security patches and the system is being aligned with best practices. Which one of the following statements is *not* a best practice for patching?
    A. Security patches should be applied as soon as possible
    B. Patches should be applied to production systems first
    C. Patches should be thoroughly tested for unintended consequences
    D. Patches should follow a change management process

Answer: **B**

Explanation: Prior to deploying patches in production, they should be applied in test environments. The security patches must be applied as soon as possible and must be tested carefully. Also, the patches should be applied through the organization's normal change management process.

164. The activities of an attacker who compromised a system on Gavin's network was traced. With this, Gavin was able to determine that the credentials belonging to a janitor have been used by the attacker. Some strange commands with very long strings of text was entered and then the attacker began using the sudo command to carry out other actions. What attack appears to have taken place?
    A. Privilege Escalation
    B. Phishing
    C. Social Engineering
    D. Session Hijacking

Answer: **A**

Explanation: A buffer overflow attack is pointed out by the use of very long query strings. The string was used to compromise a local application to perform privilege escalation. The elevated privileges after the buffer overflow attack are confirmed by the sudo command. The possible ways that the attacker compromised the janitor's account originally include phishing, social engineering, and session hijacking. However, any of these cannot be considered as a particular attack.

165. Under the data classification scheme of the U.S. government, which of the following is the lowest level of classified information?

A. Private
B. Top Secret
C. Confidential
D. Secret

Answer: **C**

Explanation: Under the U.S. government information classification scheme, the classification levels in ascending order are Confidential, Secret, and Top Secret. Private is not included in a government classification.

166. Roger is a cybersecurity analyst at a bank. A forensic analysis of the workstation belonging to an IT staff member was conducted by him as it was reported that some of the members were engaged in in illicit activity. The cookies from user sessions were being captured and stored as they were sent between backend systems. What might be the type of attack that had been conducted?

A. Privilege Escalation
B. Covert Channel
C. Session Hijacking
D. SQL Injection

Answer: **C**

Explanation: The most frequent reason could be that an employee might be storing cookies in order to use the sessions IDs stored in those cookies to engage in a session hijacking attack. This would allow an attacker to impersonate the user and conduct financial transactions.

167. From the intrusion prevention system of Tammy's organization, security alerts are being reviewed and a far too many alerts were found to be reviewed. In order to correlate with her IPS records to achieve the best results, what information source might she use?

A. Vulnerability Scans

B. Firewall Rules
C. Port Scans
D. IDS Logs

Answer: **A**

Explanation: The results of vulnerability scans can be correlated with Tammy's IPS alerts. The correlation is carried out to determine whether the systems that is being targeted in attacks against her network are vulnerable to the attempted exploits. The redundant information would be present in the IDS logs rather than correlated one. Some useful information when correlated with IPS alerts may be provided with port scans and firewall rules, but the similar information enhanced with the actual vulnerabilities on particular systems would be provided only by the results of vulnerability scans.

168. Jay, being a CISO, is responsible for conducting periodic reviews of his organization's information security policy. The policy has undergone several minor revisions after audits and assessments and was written three years ago. Given are the frequencies to conduct formal reviews of the policy. Which one of the following would be the most reasonable?

A. Monthly
B. Quarterly
C. Annually
D. Every five years

Answer: **C**

Explanation: An industry standard of security policies are annual reviews. These reviews are sufficient unless there are special circumstances. The circumstances include a new policy or major changes in the environment whereas, by waiting five years for the review, important changes in the environment can be missed out.

169. A company runs a website that allows public postings hired Alan as a cybersecurity analyst. He received complaints from the users that the website is showing them pop-up messages asking for their passwords that do not seem legitimate. Also, there has been an uptick in compromised user accounts at the same time. Against Alan's website, what is the type of attack that is likely occurring?

A. SQL Injection

B. Cross-site Scripting
C. Cross-site Request Forgery
D. Rootkit

Answer: **B**

Explanation: All of the hallmarks of a cross-site scripting attack are being indicated in the scenario given in this question. The messages containing HTML code are allowed to be posted by the site in the most likely case and input validation to remove scripts from that code is not performed. A cross-site script creates a pop-up window that is being used by the attacker and the information is then being used to compromise accounts.

170. An intrusion prevention system is being deployed by Hank in order to protect his organization's network. His requirements would most likely be met by which one of the following tools?

A. Snort
B. Burp
C. Sourcefire
D. Bro

Answer: **B**

Explanation: Snort, Sourcefire, and Bro are all intrusion detection and prevention systems while Burp is a web interception proxy, not an intrusion prevention system.

171. In a request for an exception to security policy, which one of the following items is *not* normally included?

A. Description of a compensating control
B. Description of the risks associated with the exception
C. Proposed revision to the security policy
D. Business justification for the exception

Answer: **C**

Explanation: A proposed revision to the policy would not be included in the requests for an exception to a security policy. Due to the specific technical and/or business requirements, exceptions are documented variances from the policy. The original policy is not being altered by them, which remains in force for systems not covered by the exception.

172. Provisions for removing user access upon termination resides in which one of the following policy?

A. Data Ownership
B. Data Classification
C. Data Retention
D. Account Management

Answer: **D**

Explanation: The account life cycle from provisioning through active use and decommissioning is described in the Account Management Policies, it also includes the removal of account access upon termination. The ownership of information created or used by the organization is clearly stated in the Data ownership policies. The classification structure used by the organization and the process used to properly assign classifications to data is described in data classification policies. Information that the organization should maintain is outlined in the data retention policies.

173. A network connectivity issue is being troubleshot by Johann and the path that packets follow from his system to a remote host is being determined. Which tool would best assist him with this task?

A. ping
B. netstat
C. tracert
D. ipconfig

Answer: **C**

Explanation: The path of packet flow between two systems over a network is identified by the tracert (or traceroute) command. The potential trouble points requiring further investigation could be identified by Johann using this command.

174. Which one of the following is an incorrect statement about web proxy servers?

A. Web proxy servers decrease the speed of loading web pages
B. Web proxy servers reduce network traffic
C. Web proxy servers can filter malicious content
D. Web proxy servers can enforce content restrictions

Answer: **A**

Explanation: The speed of loading web pages by creating local caches of those pages is actually increased by web proxy servers that prevents the repeated trips out to remote internet servers. The network traffic is then reduced by them for the same reason. Web proxies may also serve as content filters, blocking both malicious traffic and traffic that violates content policies.

175. In order to provide an authentication on an open network, which one of the following protocols is best suited?

A. TACACS
B. RADIUS
C. TACACS+
D. Kerberos

Answer: **D**

Explanation: An automatic protection for authentication traffic is only provided in Kerberos. TACACS+ is considered unsafe in most circumstances as it is outdated. The TACACS+ should be used on secure networks only if it mandatory. RADIUS can be secured but is not secure by default.

176. The security of a Windows server is being assessed by Eric. He also assist the users in identifying who has access to a shared file directory. What would be the Sysinternals tool that can assist him with this task?

A. AutoRuns
B. SDelete
C. Sysmon
D. AccessEnum

Answer: **D**

Explanation: The system access is enumerated by AccessEnum tool. A view of a person who is able to access files, directories, and other objects is provided with this tool. The programs that starts at login or system boot are shown in AutoRuns. SDelete is a secure file deletion utility. The monitoring of processes and administrator's activity in a searchable manner are possibly allowed with Sysmon.

177. The governance structures for enterprise architecture in Laura's organization is being improved. The effort is to increase the communication between the architects and the security team. Laura is operating which of the four domains in the TOGAF framework?

A. Business Architecture
B. Application Architecture
C. Data Architecture
D. Technical Architecture

Answer: **A**

Explanation: Governance and organization is defined in Business Architecture. It explains the interaction between enterprise architecture and business strategy. The applications and systems that an organization deploys, their relation to business processes, and the interactions between those systems are included in application architecture. The organization's approach to storing and managing information assets is provided in data architecture. The infrastructure needed to support the other architectural domains are described in technical architecture.

178. A reputable source of information about software vulnerabilities, that was updated recently, was found by Colin. His requirements would be best met by which one of the following sources?

A. OWASP
B. SANS
C. Microsoft
D. Google

Answer: **A**

Explanation: A listing of common application vulnerabilities is maintained in The Open Web Application Security Project (OWASP). A similar list is maintained also in SANS but its updating stopped in 2011. A similar list is not published with Microsoft and Google.

179. A SIEM is to be deployed in Lou's organization but no funding's are available to purchase a commercial product. An open source licensing model is used by which one of the following SIEMs?

A. AlienVault
B. QRadar
C. ArcSight
D. OSSIM

Answer: **D**

Explanation: AlienVault makes an open source SIEM called OSSIM. Information from a wide variety of open source security tools is pulled by AlienVault whereas QRadar, ArcSight, and AlienVault are all examples of commercial SIEM solutions.

180. The acquisition of a software testing package allowing programmers to provide their source code as input is taken under consideration by Bruce. The code is analyzed and any potential security issues in the code based upon that analysis are identified by the package. What type of analysis is the package performing?

A. Static Analysis
B. Fuzzing
C. Dynamic Analysis
D. Fault Injection

Answer: **A**

Explanation: The manual or automated techniques that review the source code without executing it is provided by Static Analysis. The dynamic analysis that execute the code and attempt to induce flaws includes fuzzing and fault injection.

181. What element should occupy the middle blank circle in the center of TOGAF Architecture Development Model shown below?

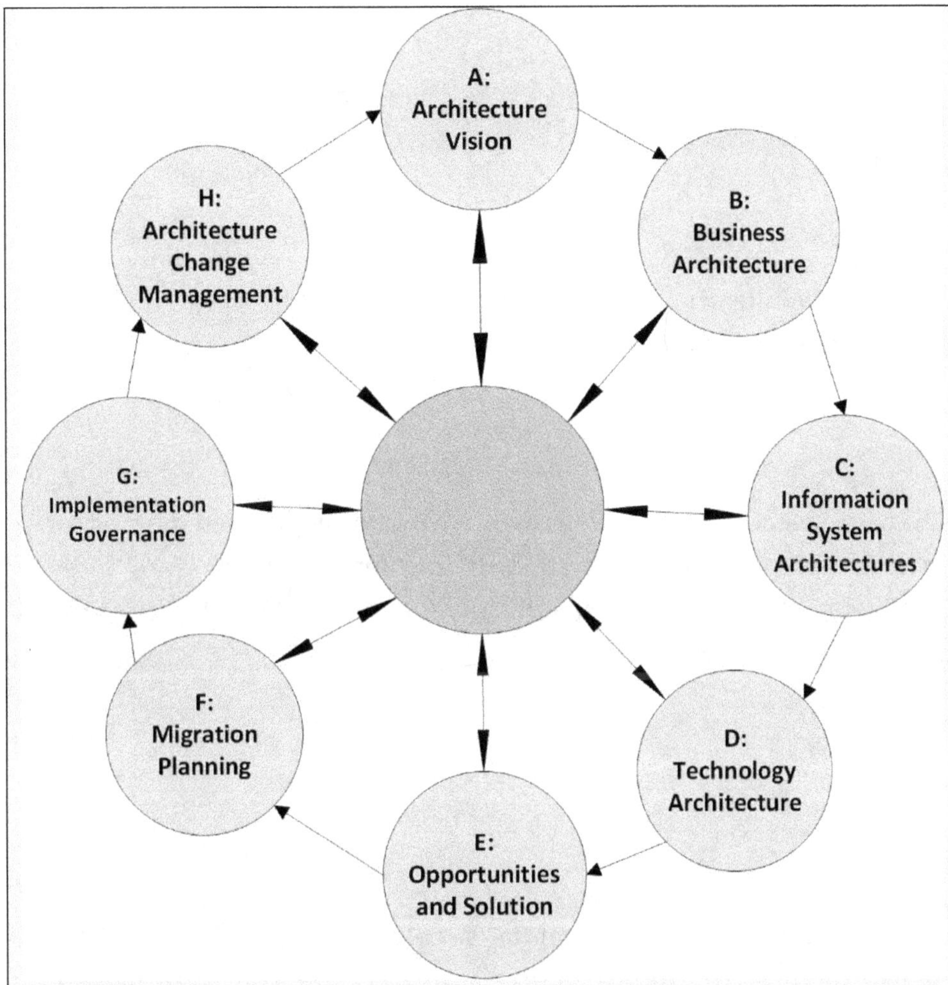

A. Security
B. Architecture
C. Requirements
D. Controls

Answer: **C**

Explanation: Requirements is the center part of the TOGAF Architecture Development Model. Each of the other phases of the model are included in the requirements.

182. To collect the information from systems running a specific operating system only, which one of the following vulnerability scanning tools is used?

A. Nikto
B. OpenVAS
C. MBSA
D. Qualys

Answer: **C**

Explanation: The Microsoft Baseline Security Analyzer (MBSA) works only with Microsoft operating systems. While the other products listed would only allow the scanning systems running any operating system.

183. Brenda would like to select a tool that assists with the automated testing of applications that she developed. A tool that will automatically generate large volumes of inputs to feed to the software is specifically looked for. Which one of the following tools would best meet her needs?

A. Peach Fuzzer
B. Burp
C. ZAP
D. ModSecurity

Answer: **A**

Explanation: A Fuzzer is the type of tool that Brenda is seeking for. The Peach Fuzzer is a solution that meets these requirements. Burp and ZAP are the examples of interception proxies. While ModSecurity is a web application firewall tool.

184. A law enforcement agency on a digital forensic investigation has hired Warren as a forensic analyst. The company intends to perform a forensic analysis of a phone that was obtained from a suspect. For the mobile forensics, which one of the following tools is designed specifically?

A. FTK
B. EnCase
C. Cellebrite
D. Helix

Answer: **C**

Explanation: Although the forensic analysis on mobile devices can be performed by using all of these tools, Cellebrite is a purpose-built tool and has been designed specifically for mobile forensics.

185. A company hosting several web applications has a security analyst named as Crystal. A tool that runs within Crystal's browser is intended to be identified that will allow her to interactively modify session values during a live session. Crystal's requirements are met by which one of the following tools?

A. Tamper Data
B. Acunetix
C. Zap
D. Burp

Answer: **A**

Explanation: The session values would be modified by all of the tools listed in the question. Out of these tools, only Tamper Data is a browser plug-in. It works within the Firefox browser and the session data of user is modified by it before it is submitted to a web server.

186. A Linux system was connected with Terrence remotely and the active network connections on the system is being determined. Select one of the following command that can be used to discover this information most easily?

A. ifconfig
B. tcpdump
C. iptables
D. ipconfig

Answer: **A**

Explanation: The information about network interfaces on a Linux system is displayed by the ifconfig command. Similar information is displayed on Windows systems by using the ipconfig command. tcpdump is a packet capture tool and iptables is a Linux firewall.

187. The forensic tools are being evaluated by Kieran and the use of an open source forensic suite would like to be taken under consideration. His requirements would

be met with which one of the following toolkits?

A. FTK
B. EnCase
C. SIFT
D. Helix

Answer: **C**

Explanation: An Ubuntu-based set of open source forensics tools is the SANS Investigative Forensics Toolkit (SIFT). While FTK, EnCase, and Helix are all commercial forensic toolkits.

188. A new security appliance is installed on Sam's network recently as part of a managed service deployment. The appliance is controlled by the vendor and Sam is unable to log into it or configure it. Whether the necessary security updates for the underlying operating system is received by the appliance is what the Sam is concerned about. Which one of the following is the best control that Sam can implement to alleviate his concern?

A. Configuration Management
B. Vulnerability Scanning
C. Intrusion Prevention
D. Automatic Updates

Answer: **B**

Explanation: Although the configuration management or automated patching would address this issue, Sam does not have the ability to log into the device, these are not feasible approaches. A layer of security is added by the intrusion prevention, but the issue of operating system patching are not addressed by it. Sam is allowed to detect missing patches and follow up with the vendor by using the vulnerability scanning.

189. A dispute between two different units in Thomas's business is found. These units appeared to be arguing over whether one unit may analyze data collected by the other. The guidance on this issue resides in which of following type of policies?

A. Data Ownership Policy
B. Data Classification Policy
C. Data Retention Policy

D. Account Management Policy

Answer: **A**

Explanation: The ownership of information created or used by the organization is clearly stated in the Data Ownership Policies. The classification structure used by the organization and the process used to properly assign classifications to data are described in data classification policies. The information that the organization will maintain is outlined in data retention policies. In this policy the length of time different categories of information will be retained prior to destruction. The account life cycle from provisioning through active use and decommissioning is described in the account management policies.

190. To gather the evidence in a forensic investigation, which one of the following tools is *not* typically used?

A. FTK
B. EnCase
C. Helix
D. Burp

Answer: **D**

Explanation: Burp is used in penetration testing and web application testing. It is an interception proxy. While FTK, EnCase, and Helix are all examples of forensic suites.

191. A cybersecurity breach taking place on one of the Linux servers of Renee's organization is being investigated. As the server log files are analyzed, she determined that access to an account belonging to an administrative assistant was given to the attacker. The account was determined as compromised through a social engineering attack. A few unusual-looking commands entered by the user are also shown in the log files. After seeing these commands, Renee then began issuing administrative commands to the server. What type of attack most likely took place?

A. Man-in-the-Middle
B. Buffer Overflow
C. Privilege Escalation
D. LDAP Injection

Answer: **C**

Explanation: The occurrence of a privilege escalation attack is taken place due to the fact that the user is connected with an account belonging to an administrative assistant. The user is then able to execute administrative commands.

192. A new data mining system is being designed by Carla. The access control logs for signs of unusual login attempts will be analyzed using this system. Any logins that are suspicious will automatically be locked out of the system. What type of control is being designed by Carla?
   A. Physical Control
   B. Logical Control
   C. Administrative Control
   D. Compensating Control

Answer: **B**

Explanation: The confidentiality, integrity, and availability in the digital space are enforced by Logical Controls. They are technical controls. Physical controls are security controls. The physical world gets impacted by these controls. To implement sound security management practices, organizations follow the procedural mechanisms called the Administrative controls. No indication is given for this control that they are designed to compensate for a control gap.

193. Network segmentation is not typically implemented by using which one of the following technologies?
   A. Host Firewall
   B. Network Firewall
   C. VLAN Tagging
   D. Routers and Switches

Answer: **A**

Explanation: Host firewalls cannot be used to implement network segmentation as they operate at the individual system level. For implementing the network segmentation, routers and switches may be used either physically separating networks or implementing VLAN tagging. For the segmentation of networks into different zones, the network firewalls may also be used.

194. A traceroute command is run by Maddox to determine the network path between his system and Amazon's web server. The partial results that he received are shown in the figure, the server hosting the Amazon's website has which one of the following IP addresses?

```
traceroute to d3ag4hukkh62yn.cloudfront.net (52.84.61.25), 64 hops max, 52 byte packets
 1  192.168.1.1 (192.168.1.1)  1.277 ms  0.826 ms  0.831 ms
 2  10.179.160.1 (10.179.160.1)  15.040 ms  11.744 ms  11.822 ms
 3  172.30.35.33 (172.30.35.33)  21.534 ms  18.069 ms  17.193 ms
 4  68-66-73-118.client.mchsi.com (68.66.73.118)  18.075 ms  19.740 ms  19.949 ms
 5  68-66-73-122.client.mchsi.com (68.66.73.122)  30.204 ms  19.967 ms  25.860 ms
 6  52.95.217.136 (52.95.217.136)  19.344 ms  19.719 ms  29.578 ms
 7  52.95.62.84 (52.95.62.84)  20.400 ms
    52.95.62.36 (52.95.62.36)  26.577 ms  18.650 ms
 8  52.95.62.111 (52.95.62.111)  22.613 ms
    52.95.62.63 (52.95.62.63)  20.346 ms
    52.95.62.125 (52.95.62.125)  19.759 ms
 9  54.239.42.59 (54.239.42.59)  20.141 ms
    54.239.43.211 (54.239.43.211)  32.133 ms
    54.239.42.59 (54.239.42.59)  19.903 ms
10  52.95.63.193 (52.95.63.193)  22.677 ms
    52.95.63.195 (52.95.63.195)  18.146 ms  19.960 ms
11  * * *
12  * * *
13  * * *
14  * * *
15  * * *
16  * * *
17  * * *
18  * * *
```

A. 192.168.1.1
B. 52.84.61.25
C. 52.95.63.195
D. 68.66.73.118

Answer: **B**

Explanation: In the first line of the results, you can see the destination of the traceroute; traceroute to d3ag4hukkh62yn.cloudfront.net (52.84.61.25), 64 hops max, 52 byte packets.

195. Which one of the following is the IP address for the Maddox's default gateway?

A. 192.168.1.1
B. 10.179.1.1
C. 172.30.35.33
D. 10.179.160.1

Answer: **A**

Explanation: The first hop in the traceroute results will indicate the address of the default gateway on Maddox's system. In this case, it is 192.168.1.1.

196. On the public internet that this traffic is passing through, what is the first IP address?

A. 192.168.1.1
B. 172.30.35.33
C. 52.95.63.195
D. 68.66.73.118

Answer: **D**

Explanation: In the traceroute results, the first three IP addresses are all private IP addresses, that indicates the systems are on Maddox's local network. 68.66.73.118 is the first public address that appears on the list.

197. In a data retention policy, which one of the following elements is the *least* likely to be found?

A. Minimum retention period for data
B. Maximum retention period for data
C. Description of information to retain
D. Classification of information elements

Answer: **D**

Explanation: The information that organizations maintain is described in the data retention policies and the length of time different categories of information will be retained prior to destruction. Data retention policies includes both minimum and maximum retention periods. The data classification policy covers the classification of data.

198. From the following options, which one is not an example of a physical security control?

A. Network Firewall
B. Door Lock
C. Fire Suppression System

D. Biometric Door Controller

Answer: **A**

Explanation: The controls impacting the physical world are the physical security controls. This criterion includes the door locks, biometric door controllers, and fire suppression systems. The network-based attacks are prevented network firewalls and are an example of a logical/technical control.

199. An application called Orizon is maintain by the Open Web Application Security Project (OWASP). Java classes are reviewed by this application and the potential security flaws are identified. What type of tool is Orizon?

A. Fuzzer
B. Static Code Analyzer
C. Web Application Assessor
D. Fault Injector

Answer: **B**

Explanation: Orizon performs a review of Java classes as stated in the question that indicates it is performing a source code review. The static code analyzers are the category that groups the techniques to perform source code review. The other testing techniques that has been listed in the question are all examples of dynamic code analysis. In the dynamic code analysis, the testing application actually executes the code.

200. The details about the flow of information in a complex system would be provided in which one of the following security architectural views?

A. Technical View
B. Logical View
C. Firewall View
D. Operational View

Answer: **D**

Explanation: The way a function is performed and the task to be accomplished by it would be described in the operational view. The way the information flows in a system is typically shown in this view. The technologies, settings, and configurations used in an architecture are enforced by the technical view. The logical view describes how systems interconnect. The firewall view is not a standard architectural view.

201. An evaluation of the application by end users is typically involved in which one of the following testing types?
   A. Stress Testing
   B. Fuzz Testing
   C. Acceptance Testing
   D. Regression Testing

Answer: **C**

Explanation: The last type of testing performed is typically the User Acceptance Testing (UAT) and it is generally the only software testing that involves end users.

202. Authentication for APIs is provided by Susan using an open standard. If she intends to connect to existing cloud service provider partners, which of the following protocols is best suited to her requirement?
   A. RADIUS
   B. SAML
   C. OAuth
   D. TACACS+

Answer: **C**

Explanation: In order to provide authentication for APIs, the OAuth is commonly used with many service providers who support it are allowed with OAuth. AAA services for network devices are more commonly provided with RADIUS and TACACS+, while single sign-on to websites is often provided by SAML that is an XML-based standard.

203. An authentication infrastructure is being designed by Nick and an authentication protocol is required to be run over an insecure network without using the additional encryption services. For this situation, which one of the following protocols is the most appropriate?
   A. RADIUS
   B. TACACS
   C. TACACS+
   D. Kerberos

Answer: **D**

Explanation: The insecure networks make the use of the Kerberos protocol design and strong encryption to protect authentication traffic is used in it. Whereas RADIUS, TACACS, and TACACS+ all contain vulnerabilities that require the use of additional encryption to protect their traffic.

204. The security of Francine's organization's wireless networks would like to be assessed. For this task, which one of the following network security tools would be best suited?

A. Wireshark
B. tcpdump
C. nmap
D. aircrack-ng

Answer: **D**

Explanation: A suite of wireless security tools is aircrack-ng. It suits Francine's Wi-Fi security assessment perfectly.

205. A company having a network security standard that requires the collection and storage of NetFlow logs from all data center networks hires Miguel for the work. A new data center network is commissioned but the NetFlow logs for the first six months of operation could not be collected due to technical constraints. To serve as a compensating control for the lack of NetFlow information, which one of the following data sources is best suited?

A. Router Logs
B. Firewall Logs
C. Switch Logs
D. IPS Logs

Answer: **B**

Explanation: The information similar to that contained in NetFlow records are typically given in Firewall Logs. the firewall does not always have the same access to network traffic because of the switches and routers that generate NetFlow information. While not a complete substitute, firewall logs do offer a good compensating control for the lack of NetFlow records. The traffic records in their standard logs are not typically recorded in the Routers and switches. This is the function of NetFlow, which is unavailable on this network. The routine traffic information is not recorded by Intrusion Prevention Systems (IPS).

206. An alarm is configured by Ken to alert him whenever an event is recorded to syslog having a critical severity level. For the severity in his alert, what value should he use that corresponds to critical messages?

A. 0
B. 2
C. 5
D. 7

Answer: **B**

Explanation: The ranges of Syslog severity is from 0 (emergency) down to 7 (debug). The lower number in this range represents higher severities. A critical severity error is corresponded with the value of 2.

207. The contents of a compromised server are being reviewed by Patrick and the installation of an intruder, a tool called John the Ripper, is determined. What is the purpose of this tool?

A. Stealing copyrighted media content
B. Cracking passwords
C. Monitoring network traffic
D. Launching DDoS attacks

Answer: **B**

Explanation: A password cracking tool used to retrieve plain-text passwords from where the hashed passwords are stored is called John the Ripper.

208. While hiding his or her presence on the system, what type of malicious software might an attacker use in an attempt to maintain access to a system?

A. Rootkit
B. Worm
C. Trojan horse
D. Virus

Answer: **A**

Explanation: Multiple malicious software tools are combined in Rootkits to provide continued access to a system while their own existence is kept hidden. A full suite of system security practices is required in the fighting rootkits, ranging from proper patching and layered security design to anti-malware techniques such as whitelisting, heuristic detection, and malicious software detection tools.

209. As Cody seeks to determine the identity of the individual responsible for the installation of the software, which one of the following sources of information would be most useful?

A. Server Logs
B. Netflow Records
C. Kerberos Logs
D. IPS Logs

Answer: **A**

Explanation: Although the clues to the identity of the individual who installed the software may be provided with All of the information sources listed in the question, the server logs are likely to contain records of software installation and associate them with a user ID. The most direct answer to Cody's question in the shortest possible time period can be easily provided by this source.

210. What type of control should Cody consider implementing to identify similar issues in the future more quickly?

A. Intrusion Prevention
B. Authentication Anomaly Detection
C. Vulnerability Scanning
D. Configuration Management

Answer: **D**

Explanation: The installation of new software is easily detected by the Configuration management tools. It helps the analysts to identify cases of unauthorized software installation quickly. This issue is detected by authentication anomaly detection and intrusion prevention controls as the employee are authorized to connect to server and the authorized access privileges are being simply misused.

211. Fuzz testing is being conducted by using Peach Fuzzer that is a common input fuzzing tool. Vincent is carrying out this testing process. Functionality that is formerly included in the Untidy fuzzer project is incorporated with Peach Fuzzer. Which one of the following sources is Vincent LEAST likely to be able to fuzz with this product?

A. Web Application Input
B. XML
C. TCP/IP
D. Firewall Rules

Answer: **D**

Explanation: An input to an application is manipulated dynamically as part of a Fuzz testing in an effort to induce a flaw. The places where a web application does not perform proper input validation are easily detected by this technique. It can also be used against XML input, TCP/IP communications and other protocols. It is not commonly used against firewall rules. The mentioning of Untidy fuzzer in this question should be noticed. The product was once an XML fuzzer that no longer exists due to the fact that it was folded into the Peach fuzzing tool.

212. The software development team for the Lynda's organization is being advised for the inclusion of security best practices in their SDLC, as Lynda herself is a security professional. She consults the Center for Internet Security's system design recommendations. Information that is helpful to her consulting effort is likely to reside in which one of the following control categories?

A. Inventory of authorized and unauthorized devices
B. Controlled use of administrative privileges
C. Application software security
D. Malware defenses

Answer: **C**

Explanation: In spite of the fact that all of these control documents may contain information helpful to Lynda, the information relevant to incorporating security into the SDLC resides in the application software security control.

213. Which of the following does an Ethical Hacker require to penetrate a system?

A. Training
B. Permission
C. Planning
D. Nothing

Answer: **B**

Explanation: Ethical Hackers always require legal permission.

214. If you have been hired to perform an attack against a target system to find and exploit vulnerabilities, what type of hacker are you?

A. Gray Hat
B. Black Hat
C. White Hat
D. Red Hat

Answer: **C**

Explanation: White Hat Hackers always have legal permission to perform penetration testing against a target system.

215. A penetration test is required for which of the following reasons? (Choose 2)

A. Troubleshooting network issues
B. Finding vulnerabilities
C. Performing an audit
D. Monitoring performance

Answer: **B & C**

Explanation: Penetration testing is required in an environment to perform an audit, find vulnerabilities and exploit them to address them before an attacker reaches them.

216. Vulnerability analysis is basically ____________________.

A. Monitoring for threats
B. Disclosure, scope & prioritization of vulnerabilities

C. Defending techniques from vulnerabilities
D. Security application

Answer: **B**

Explanation: A vulnerability assessment is a process of identifying, quantifying, and prioritizing (or ranking) the vulnerabilities in a system.

217. The term "Vulnerability" refers to ______________.

A. A Virus
B. A Malware
C. An Attack
D. A Weakness

Answer: **D**

Explanation: The vulnerability is a weak point or loophole in any system or network, which can be exploited by an attacker.

218. To extract information regarding domain name registration, which of the following is the most appropriate?

A. Whois Lookup
B. DNS Lookup
C. Maltego
D. Recong-ng

Answer: **A**

Explanation: "WHOIS" helps to gain information regarding domain name, ownership information. IP Address, Netblock data, Domain Name Servers and other information. WHOIS database is maintained by Regional Internet Registries (RIR).

219. Which of the following tools is capable of performing a customized scan?

A. Nmap
B. Wireshark
C. Netcraft
D. Airpcap

Answer: **A**

Explanation: Nmap in a nutshell, offers host discovery, port discovery, service discovery, operating system version information, hardware (MAC) address information, service version detection, vulnerability & exploit detection.

220. Which one of the following is not an example of SNMP Manager software?

A. PRTG
B. SolarWinds
C. OPManager
D. Wireshark

Answer: **D**

Explanation: Wireshark is not an example of SNMP Manager software. It is the most popular, widely used Network Protocol Analyzer tool across commercial, governmental, non-profit and educational organizations.

221. Which of the following is not a Vulnerability Scanning tool?

A. Nessus
B. GFI LanGuard
C. Qualys Scan
D. Wireshark

Answer: **D**

Explanation: Wireshark is the most popular, widely used Network Protocol Analyzer tool across commercial, governmental, non-profit and educational organizations. It is a free, open source tool available for Windows, Linux, MAC, BSD, Solaris and other platforms natively.

222. A Phishing Attack is performed over ______________.

A. Messages
B. Phone Calls
C. Emails
D. File Sharing

Answer: **C**

Explanation: Phishing process is a technique in which fake email, which looks like legitimate email is sent to a target host. When the recipient opens the link, he is enticed for providing information.

223. To defend against phishing attack, the necessary step to take is ____________.

A. Spam Filtering
B. Traffic Monitoring
C. Email Tracking
D. Education & Training

Answer: **A**

Explanation: Spam Filtering is a necessary step to avoid phishing emails, which reduces the threat of unintentional clicking on spam emails.

224. An attack, which denies the services, and where resources become unavailable for legitimate users is known as:

A. DoS Attack
B. Application Layer Attack
C. SQL Injection
D. Network Layer Attack

Answer: **A**

Explanation: Denial of Service (DoS) is a type of attack, in which service offered by a system or a network is denied. Services may be denied, reducing the functionality or preventing the access to the resources even to the legitimate users.

225. Which statement defines Session Hijacking most accurately?

A. Stealing a user's login information to impersonate a legitimate user to access resources from the server
B. Stealing legitimate session credentials to take over an authenticated legitimate session
C. Stealing Session ID from Cookies
D. Hijacking of Web Application's session

Answer: **B**

Explanation: In Session Hijacking, the attacker intercepts the session and takes over the legitimate authenticated session. When a session authentication process is complete, and the user is authorized to use resources such as web services, TCP communication or others, the attacker takes advantage of this authenticated session and places himself in between the authenticated user and the host.

226. Which one of the following is a Patch Management Tool?

A. Microsoft Baseline Security Analyzer
B. Microsoft Network Monitor
C. Syshunt Hybrid
D. SolarWinds SIEM Tool

Answer: **A**

Explanation: The Microsoft Baseline Security Analyzer is a Windows-based Patch management tool powered by Microsoft. MBSA identifies the missing security updates and common security misconfigurations.

227. Which of the following is an example of SaaS?

A. Cisco WebEx
B. Cisco Metapod
C. Amazon EC2
D. Microsoft Azure

Answer: **A**

Explanation: Software as a Service (SaaS) is one of the most popular types of Cloud Computing Service that is most widely used. On-demand software is centrally hosted to be accessible by users using client via browsers. An example of SaaS is office software such as office 365, Cisco WebEx, Citrix GoToMeeting, Google Apps, messaging software, DBMS, CAD, ERP, HRM, etc.

228. Which of the following statement is the appropriate definition of Malware?

A. Malware are Viruses
B. Malware are Malicious Software
C. Malware are Trojans
D. Malware are Infected Files

Answer: **B**

Explanation: Malware is abbreviated from the term Malicious Software. The term malware is an umbrella term, which defines a wide variety of potentially harmful software. This malicious software is specially designed for gaining access to target machines, stealing information and harming the target system.

229. Which of the following does not belongs to the virus?

A. Replication
B. Propagation
C. Requires trigger to infect
D. Backdoor

Answer: **D**

Explanation: The virus is a self-replicating program; it is capable of producing multiple copies of itself by attaching with another program of any format. These viruses can be executed as soon as they are downloaded, it may wait for the host to execute them as well as be in sleep for a predetermined time. The major characteristics of viruses are:

A. Infecting other files
B. Alteration of data
C. Transformation
D. Corruption
E. Encryption
F. Self-Replication

230. Which of the following does not belongs to Trojan deployment?

A. Trojan Construction Kit
B. Dropper
C. Wrapper
D. Sniffers

Answer: **D**

Explanation: Trojan Deployment includes the following steps:

A. Create a Trojan using Trojan Construction Kit
B. Create a Dropper
C. Create a Wrapper
D. Propagate the Trojan
E. Execute the Dropper

231. Which one of the following is a phase of hacking?
   A. Scanning
   B. Maintaining Access
   C. Clearing Tracks
   D. All of the above

Answer: **D**

Explanation: There are five phases of hacking:
   A. Reconnaissance
   B. Scanning
   C. Gaining Access
   D. Maintaining Access
   E. Clearing Tracks

232. Select one of the following that describes an attacker who goes after a target to draw attention to a cause?
   A. Terrorist
   B. Criminal
   C. Hacktivist
   D. Script kiddie

Answer: **C**

Explanation: Hacktivists draw the attention to target to deliver a message or promoting an agenda.

233. The term hacktivism refers to ______________________.
   A. Utilization of PCs
   B. Utilization of Software's
   C. Utilization of Networks
   D. Utilization of Security

Answer: **A**

Explanation: The term hacktivism refers to utilization of PCs.

234. Select one of the following tool that is used to scan a Host.
   A. Nessus
   B. Nikto
   C. Nmap
   D. SQL map

Answer: **C**

Explanation: Nmap tool is used to scan a Host.

235. How many types of scans are there?
   A. Three
   B. Four
   C. Five
   D. Six

Answer: **B**

Explanation: There are four types of scans, which are as follows:

   A. Full Scan
   B. Stealth Scan
   C. Discovery Scan
   D. Compliance Scan

236. Which one of the following is not a Vulnerability Scanning tool?
   A. Nessus
   B. GFI LanGuard
   C. Qualys Scan
   D. Wireshark

Answer: **D**

Explanation: Wireshark is the most popular, widely used Network Protocol Analyzer tool across commercial, governmental, non-profit, and educational organizations. It is a free, open source tool available for Windows, Linux, MAC, BSD, Solaris, and other platforms natively.

237. Which policy outlines the information that an organization needs to maintain?
   A. Account Management Policy
   B. Data Retention Policy
   C. Data Classification Policy
   D. Data Ownership Policy

Answer: **B**

Explanation: The information that an organization needs to maintain is outlined in Data Retention Policy.

238. The formal reviews of security program or specific compliance issues of an organization is called _______________.
   A. Evaluation
   B. Audits
   C. Maturity Model
   D. Assessment

Answer: **B**

Explanation: The formal reviews of security program or specific compliance issues of an organization are basically carried out in Audits.

239. In which of the following attacks, the identity of a legitimate user is taken by an attacker?
   A. Man-in-the-Middle
   B. Impersonation
   C. Session hijack
   D. Privilege Escalation

Answer: **B**

Explanation: In the impersonation attack the identity of a legitimate user is taken by an attacker.

240. A command-line vulnerability scanner used for scanning the webserver for the

dangerous files/CGI's and as well as websites and virtual hosts for known security vulnerabilities is called ________________.

A. Burp Suite
B. Nikto
C. Hydra
D. John the Ripper

Answer: **B**

Explanation: The Nikto scanner is a security tool for testing many security vulnerabilities including misconfigured services, dangerous files, vulnerable scripts, and other issues. It is a popular tool that is used by many penetration testers for security analyses.

241. Select the method of extracting the password to gain authorized access to the target system in the guise of a legitimate user.

A. Filtering
B. Password Cracking
C. Vulnerability Scanning
D. Scripting

Answer: **B**

Explanation: Password Cracking is the method of extracting the password to gain authorized access to the target system in the guise of a legitimate user.

242. Biometric authentication technology fits into which of the following categories of multifactor authentication? (More than one answer)

A. Something you are
B. Something you know
C. Something you have
D. Somewhere you are

Answer: **A, B, C**

Explanation: There are three different categories of multifactor authentication:

- Something you are

- Something you know
- Something you have

243. To query a data as part of a foot printing or reconnaissance exercise provided by organizations like the American Registry for Internet Numbers (ARIN), which of the following tools is best suited?
    A. nmap
    B. whois
    C. regmon
    D. traceroute

Answer: **B**

Explanation: ARIN, the Regional Internet registries, are best queried either via their websites or using tools like Whois. Nmap is a port scanning utility, path that the packets take to a remote system is tested by traceroute, and an outdated Windows Registry tool is regmon that has been supplanted by Process Monitor.

244. One of Alice's www.hellodigi.ir scans encountered a false positive error during a vulnerability scan. What should she do about this?
    A. Use an authenticated scan, and then document the vulnerability
    B. Implement a workaround
    C. Verify that it is a false positive, and then document the exception
    D. Update the vulnerability scanner

Answer: **C**

Explanation: Upon encountering a false positive error in Alice's scans, she took the first action as to verify it. A more in-depth scan like an authenticated scan is being carried out, also the documentation is being checked, assistance from system administrators or other actions for the validation are being taken. She should document the exception so as to track it properly. For false positive vulnerabilities, implementing a workaround is not necessary. The scanner should be updated before every vulnerability scan. Although using an authenticated scan might help but all of the possibilities for validation that she may need to use are not being covered.

245. An additional evidence gathering such as information supporting legal action

would most likely be included in which of the following phase of the incident response process?

A. Preparation
B. Detection and Analysis
C. Post-Incident Activity and Reporting
D. Containment, Eradication, and Recovery

Answer: **D**

Explanation: An incident's Recovery, Containment, and Eradication phase includes steps. In these steps, the damage is limited and the occurred incident is documented. This includes identifying the attacker's potential and tools used for the attack. During this phase, the gathered information is most useful.

246. Which one of the following tools cannot be used to create a forensic disk image?

A. FTK
B. Dd
C. EnCase
D. xcopy

Answer: **D**

Explanation: Options supporting the use for forensic disk image creation are provided with FTK, EnCase, and dd. A bitwise image of a drive cannot be created with xcopy and the forensic images cannot be created by using it.

247. During a forensic investigation, Shelly is told to look for information in slack space on the drive. What would be place she is likely to look for?

A. She is likely to find file fragments from deleted files and thus she should look at unallocated space
B. The unused space where files were deleted should be looked at and the complete files hidden there should likely to be found. These files are hidden there by the individual being investigated
C. The left over unused space should be looked at and the file fragments from deleted files are likely to be found there
D. The space reserved on the drive for spare blocks should be looked for and the complete duplicated files are likely to be found there

Answer: **C**

Explanation: Slack space is the space left when a file is written. Since the space may have previously been filled by another file, file fragments are likely to exist and be recoverable. Unallocated space is space that has not been partitioned and could contain data, but looking there is not part of Shelly's task. The reserved space maintained by drives for wear leveling (for SSDs) or to replace bad blocks (for spinning disks) may contain data, but again, this was not part of her task.

248. "The current security configuration template that is applied to Windows workstation must be included in it before being deployed", which of the following document most likely includes this statement?

A. Guidelines
B. Policies
C. Standards
D. Procedures

Answer: **C**

Explanation: Standard is considered to include this statement. The high-level statements of management intent are a part of the Policies; the mandatory requirements for the policies to be carried out is provided in standards that includes statements like the one provided in the question. The step-by-step process would be included in a procedure, and a best practice or recommendation would be described in a guideline.

249. A fire suppression system is an example of which type of control?

A. Physical
B. Logical
C. Operational
D. Administrative

Answer: **A**

Explanation: Fire suppression systems are physical controls. The technical controls are part of logical controls that enforce integrity, confidentiality, and availability. Procedural controls are a part of administrative controls, and operational controls are not a type of security control as used in security design.

250. Which of the following options is best suited to implemented an authentication

protocol that is well suited to untrusted networks?

A. LDAP
B. RADIUS
C. Kerberos
D. TACACS+

Answer: **C**

Explanation: Kerberos is being run on untrusted networks and an authentication traffic is encrypted by default in the process. Both RADIUS and LDAP can be encrypted but are not encrypted by default necessarily (as an authentication mechanism, LDAP also has some limitations) TACACS+ is recommended to be run only on isolated administrative networks.

251. Which of the following is an example of operational security control?

A. Penetration Tests
B. Encryption Software
C. Antivirus Software
D. Network Firewall

Answer: **A**

Explanation: An operational security control is a part of penetration tests. Network firewalls, antivirus software, and encryption software are all examples of technical security controls.

252. A Bring Your Own Device (BYOD) policy is part of Robert's organization, and the devices connected to the network under this policy are ensured to have current antivirus software. What could be the technology he used?

A. Virtual Private Network
B. Network Segmentation
C. Network Access Control
D. Network Firewall

Answer: **C**

Explanation: The security status of devices are verified by Network Access Control (NAC) solutions. The devices are verified before being granted access to the organization's network. Devices that do not meet the minimum security standards are placed on a quarantine network until they are remediated.

253. A cybersecurity wargame exercise is being conducted. Barry's role is to attempt breaking into adversary systems. What team is he currently on?

A. Blue Team
B. Red Team
C. Black Team
D. White Team

Answer: **B**

Explanation: The attacker's role is carried out by the red team. The reconnaissance and exploitation tools are used in an attempt to gain access of the protected network.

254. By using which of the following command-line tool, the path traffic that takes to a remote system is determined?

A. routeview
B. nslookup
C. traceroute
D. Whois

Answer: **C**

Explanation: A command-line tool using ICMP to trace the route is Traceroute, or tracert on Windows systems. The route that a packet takes to a host is traced. The domain tools that includes Whois and nslookup, and routeview are not a command-line tool.

255. An information about a domain's registrar and physical location is provided in which one of the following lookup tools?

A. host
B. nslookup
C. traceroute
D. Whois

Answer: **D**

Explanation: Information including the organization's physical address, contact information, registrar, and other details are provided with Whois. IP address or hostname information will be provided with nslookup while IPv4 and IPv6 addresses as well as email service information are provided with host. The path to a remote host and the systems along with the route is being identified in traceroute attempts.

256. A system subjected to the PCI DSS compliance standard is being configured for a vulnerability scan. What is the minimum frequency required to conduct the scans?

A. Weekly
B. Quarterly
C. Monthly
D. Daily

Answer: **B**

Explanation: Vulnerability scans are required to be conducted by organizations on at least a quarterly basis. These scans are as per PCI DSS requirements. It is considered that many organizations choose to conduct scans on a much more frequent basis.

257. Bethany completed her last PCI DSS compliance scan in March, she is the vulnerability management specialist for a large retail organization. The organization's point-of-sale system was upgraded in April, and new scans were being conducted by Bethany. When must the new scan be completed?

A. December
B. Immediately
C. No scans are required
D. June

Answer: **B**

Explanation: Vulnerability scans needs to be conducted on a quarterly basis as per PCI DSS requirement, that would have Bethany's next regularly scheduled scan set for June. The scanning after any significant change in the payment card environment is also required, this would include an upgrade to the point-of-sale system. Hence, a new compliance scan must be completed by Bethany on immediate basis.

258. Which of the following term describes an organization's willingness to tolerate risk in a computing environment?

A. Risk Level
B. Risk Adaptation
C. Risk landscape
D. Risk Appetite

Answer: **D**

Explanation: The organization's willingness to tolerate risk within the environment is called the organization's risk appetite.

259. The vulnerability scanning schedules are least likely to be impacted by which one of the following factors?

A. Technical Constraints
B. Regulatory Requirements
C. Staff Availability
D. Business Constraints

Answer: **C**

Explanation: The organization's risk appetite, technical constraints, regulatory requirements, licensing limitations, and business constraint most often determines the scan schedules. Most scans do not require staff availability and are automated.

260. A vulnerability scan of a business critical system is intended to be conducted. Ryan conducts this scan using dangerous plug-ins. For the initial scan, what would be the best approach?

A. Do not run the scan to avoid disrupting the business
B. Run the scan in a test environment
C. Run the scan during business hours
D. Run the scan against production systems to achieve the most realistic results possible

Answer: **B**

Explanation: Scan should be run against a test environment by Ryan to identify likely vulnerabilities and assess whether the business activities might be disrupted by the scan itself.

261. Out of the vulnerability management life cycle's activities, which one of the following is not part of the vulnerability management life cycle?

A. Testing
B. Reporting
C. Remediation
D. Detection

Answer: **B**

Explanation: An important part of vulnerability management is reporting and communication. The three life-cycle phases are detection, remediation, and testing while reporting is not included in the life cycle.

262. Information from agents that are being operated on the target servers are incorporated in which of the vulnerability scanning approach?

A. Ongoing Scanning
B. Alerting
C. Continuous Monitoring
D. On-demand Scanning

Answer: **C**

Explanation: Data from agent-based approaches is incorporated to vulnerability detection in Continuous Monitoring. The security-related configuration changes are being reported to the vulnerability management platform as soon as they occur. It provides the ability to analyze the changes for potential vulnerabilities.

263. A new security vulnerability was recently identified by Kevin and the CVSS base score was computed as 6.5; This vulnerability falls into which of the following categories?

A. Medium
B. High

C. Critical
D. Low

Answer: **B**

Explanation: A CVSS score for Vulnerabilities that is higher than 6.0 but less than 10.0 falls into the High risk category.

264. Tara found that a vulnerability reported by the scanner did not exist as the system was actually patched and specified. What type of error occurred when the results of a vulnerability scan report were analyzed?

A. False Negative
B. True Negative
C. False Positive
D. True Positive

Answer: **C**

Explanation: When the vulnerability scanner reports a vulnerability that does not exists actually, the occurrence of a false positive error takes place.

265. Which one of the following is not an information's common source that may be correlated with vulnerability scan results?

A. Configuration Management System
B. SIEM
C. Database Tables
D. Logs

Answer: **C**

Explanation: It is unlikely that an information relevant to assessing a vulnerability scan report is kept in a database table. The relevant information is much more likely to be residing in Logs, SIEM reports, and configuration management systems.

266. Buffer-overflow is also known as ______________________________.

A. Buffer-overrun

B. Buffer-leak
C. Memory leakage
D. Data overflow

Answer: **A**

Explanation: Buffer-overflow, also known as buffer-overrun is a widespread application's coding mistake made by app developers that could be exploited by an attacker for gaining access or malfunctioning your system.

267. Which of the following vulnerability type includes the Dirty COW Attack?

A. LDAP Injection
B. Malicious Code
C. Buffer Overflow
D. Privilege Escalation

Answer: **D**

Explanation: The discovery of a Linux kernel vulnerability dubbed Dirty COW was announced by the security researchers in October 2016. This vulnerability was extremely easy to exploit and the successful attackers were provided with administrative control of affected systems.

268. Which one of the following protocols a public network is not supposed to use?

A. Telnet
B. SSH
C. SFTP
D. HTTPS

Answer: **A**

Explanation: Telnet does not make use of encryption and is an insecure protocol. All the protocols mentioned in the question are all considered as secure.

269. The connection of physical devices to a network is not typically described by using which one of the following terms?

A. IDS
B. IoT
C. SCADA
D. ICS

Answer: **A**

Explanation: A security control, called Intrusion Detection System (IDS), is used to detect network or host attacks. The Supervisory Control and Data Acquisition (SCADA) systems, Internet of Things (IoT), and Industrial Control Systems (ICS) are all associated with connecting physical world objects to a network.

270. Which one of the following attack types is most likely to occur when a message is posted by an attacker and pasted in a web forum?

A. Cross-site Scripting
B. LDAP Injection
C. SQL Injection
D. Malware Injection

Answer: **A**

Explanation: The scripting commands on a website are embedded by an attacker in a cross-site scripting (XSS) attack. These commands are executed later on by an unsuspecting visitor accessing the site.

271. Web server logs are being reviewed after occurrence of an attack and many records containing semicolons and apostrophes in queries from end users were found. What could be the suspected attack type?

A. SQL Injection
B. LDAP Injection
C. Cross-site Scripting
D. Buffer Overflow

Answer: **A**

Explanation: In an SQL injection attack, the attacker seeks to use a web application to gain access to an underlying database. Semicolons and apostrophes are characteristic of these attacks.

272. The organization's detection and analysis capabilities is being developed by Alan. A system able to combine log records from multiple sources to detect potential security incidents is being considered to put in process. Alan's security objective could be met by which of the following types of system?

A. Firewall
B. IPS
C. IDS
D. SIEM

Answer: **D**

Explanation: Log entries from multiple sources are correlated by a Security Information and Event Management (SIEM) system. It is basically used to identify potential security incidents.

273. How many types of buffer-overflow attack are there?

A. 4
B. 2
C. 5
D. 3

Answer: **B**

Explanation: There are two different types of buffer-overflow attacks. These are stack-based and heap-based buffer overflow. In both the cases, this type of exploit takes advantage of an application that waits for user's input.

274. William completed a risk assessment and determined that his network was vulnerable to hackers connecting to open ports on servers. He implemented a network firewall to reduce the likelihood of a successful attack. Which of the following risk management strategy did William choose to pursue?

A. Risk Transference
B. Risk Acceptance

C. Risk Mitigation

D. Risk Avoidance

Answer: **C**

Explanation: Any action that an organization takes to reduce the likelihood or impact of a risk is an example of risk mitigation.

275. Who is the best facilitator for a post-incident lessons-learned session?

A. Independent Facilitator

B. First Responder

C. CEO

D. CSIRT Leader

Answer: **A**

Explanation: Lessons-learned sessions are most effective when facilitated by an independent party who was not involved in the incident response effort.

276. John wants to use an active monitoring approach to test his network. Which of the following methods is appropriate?

A. Enabling SNMP

B. Pinging Remote Systems

C. Using a Protocol Analyzer

D. Collecting NetFlow Data

Answer: **B**

Explanation: Active monitoring is focused on reaching out to gather data using tools like ping and iPerf. Passive monitoring using protocol analyzers collects network traffic and router-based monitoring using SNMP, and flows gather data by receiving or collecting logged information.

277. Which of the following is not an Incident Management Process?

A. Preparation for Incident Response

B. Reporting
C. Detection and Analysis of Incident Response
D. Classification of an incident and its prioritization

Answer: **B**

Explanation: Reporting is not an incident management process. It is a responsibility of the Incident Response Team.

278. Who deploys Malwares to a system or network?

A. Criminal organizations, black hat hackers, malware developers, cyber-terrorists
B. Criminal organizations, white hat hackers, malware developers, cyber-terrorists
C. Criminal organizations, black hat hackers, software developers, cyber-terrorists
D. Criminal organizations, gray hat hackers, malware developers, Penetration testers

Answer: **A**

Explanation: Criminal-minded organizations, groups and individual cyber-terrorist groups, black hat hackers, malware developers etc. are those who can deploy malwares to any target system or network in order to deface that system.

279. Which of the following is a code injecting method used for attacking the database of a system / website?

A. HTML Injection
B. SQL Injection
C. Malicious Code Injection
D. XML Injection

Answer: **B**

Explanation: SQLi (Structured Query Language Injection) is a popular attack where SQL code is targeted or injected for breaking the web application having SQL vulnerabilities. This allows the attacker to run malicious code and take access to the database of that server.

280. Which of the following is not a wireless attack?

A. Eavesdropping
B. MAC Spoofing
C. Wireless Hijacking
D. Phishing

Answer: **D**

Explanation: Wireless attacks are malicious attacks done in wireless systems, networks or devices. Attacks on Wi-Fi network is one common example that general people know. Other such sub-types of wireless attacks are wireless authentication attack, encryption cracking and so on.

281. Which of the following is an example of physical hacking?

A. Remote unauthorized access
B. Inserting malware loaded USB to a system
C. SQL Injection on SQL vulnerable site
D. DDoS (Distributed Denial of Service) attack

Answer: **B**

Explanation: If a suspicious individual gains access to server room or into any confidential area with a malicious pen-drive loaded with malware that will get triggered automatically once inserted to the USB port of any employee's PC, such attacks come under physical hacking. That person gained unauthorized physical access to a room or organization first, then managed to get an employee's PC also, all done physically – hence it is breaching physical security

282. Select the one that is not a wireless attack.

A. Eavesdropping
B. MAC Spoofing
C. Wireless Hijacking
D. Phishing

Answer: **D**

Explanation: Wireless attacks are malicious attacks done in wireless systems, networks or devices. Attacks on Wi-Fi network is one common example that general people know. Other such sub-types of wireless attacks are wireless authentication attack, encryption cracking, etc.

283. An attempt to harm, damage or cause threat to a system or network is broadly termed as ________________________.

A. Cyber Crime
B. Cyber Attack
C. System Hijacking
D. Digital Crime

Answer: **B**

Explanation: A Cyber Attack is an umbrella term used to classify different computer & network attacks or activities such as extortion, identity theft, email hacking, digital spying, stealing hardware, mobile hacking and physical security breaching.

About Our Products

Other Network & Security related products from IPSpecialist LTD are:

- CCNA Routing & Switching Technology Workbook
- CCNA Security v2 Technology Workbook
- CCNA Service Provider Technology Workbook
- CCDA Technology Workbook
- CCDP Technology Workbook
- CCNP Route Technology Workbook
- CCNP Switch Technology Workbook
- CCNP Troubleshoot Technology Workbook
- CCNP Security SENSS Technology Workbook
- CCNP Security SIMOS Technology Workbook
- CCNP Security SITCS Technology Workbook
- CCNP Security SISAS Technology Workbook
- CompTIA Network+ Technology Workbook
- CompTIA Security+ v2 Technology Workbook
- Certified Information System Security Professional (CISSP) Technology Workbook
- CCNA CyberOps SECFND Technology Workbook
- Certified Block Chain Expert Technology Workbook
- Certified Cloud Security Professional (CCSP) Technology Workbook
- CompTIA Pentest Technology Workbook
- CompTIA A+ Core I (220-1001) Technology Workbook
- CompTIA A+ Core II (220-1002) Technology Workbook

Upcoming products are:

- CompTIA Cloud+ Technology Workbook
- CompTIA Server+ Technology Workbook

Note from the Author:

Reviews are gold to authors! If you have enjoyed this book and it helped you along certification, would you consider rating and reviewing it?

Link to Product Page:

www.ingramcontent.com/pod-product-compliance
Lightning Source LLC
LaVergne TN
LVHW081659050326
832903LV00026B/1827